CAMBRIDGE LIBRARY COLLECTION

Books of enduring scholarly value

Spiritualism and Esoteric Knowledge

Magic, superstition, the occult sciences and esoteric knowledge appear regularly in the history of ideas alongside more established academic disciplines such as philosophy, natural history and theology. Particularly fascinating are periods of rapid scientific advances such as the Renaissance or the nineteenth century which also see a burgeoning of interest in the paranormal among the educated elite. This series provides primary texts and secondary sources for social historians and cultural anthropologists working in these areas, and all who wish for a wider understanding of the diverse intellectual and spiritual movements that formed a backdrop to the academic and political achievements of their day. It ranges from works on Babylonian and Jewish magic in the ancient world, through studies of sixteenth-century topics such as Cornelius Agrippa and the rapid spread of Rosicrucianism, to nineteenth-century publications by Sir Walter Scott and Sir Arthur Conan Doyle. Subjects include astrology, mesmerism, spiritualism, theosophy, clairvoyance, and ghost-seeing, as described both by their adherents and by sceptics.

The Magical Ritual of the Sanctum Regnum

Éliphas Lévi, born Alphonse Louis Constant, (1810–75) was instrumental in the revival of Western occultism in the nineteenth century, and published several influential books on magic that are also reissued in this series. This posthumous publication (1896) is a translation by William Wynn Westcott, co-founder of the 'Hermetic Order of the Golden Dawn', of an unpublished French manuscript by Lévi, then owned by the spiritualist Edward Maitland. It includes eight of the author's drawings. Each short chapter outlines the meaning of one of the twenty-two tarot trumps and is followed by a brief editor's note describing the card's iconography and summarising interpretations (sometimes deliberately misleading) given in Lévi's earlier publications. The book ends with Kabbalistic prayers and rituals, praise of Jesus Christ as the great initiate, and a surprising assertion that Christianity has superseded ancient magic, revealing the life-long tension between Catholicism and magic in Lévi's personality and thought.

T0345421

Cambridge University Press has long been a pioneer in the reissuing of out-of-print titles from its own backlist, producing digital reprints of books that are still sought after by scholars and students but could not be reprinted economically using traditional technology. The Cambridge Library Collection extends this activity to a wider range of books which are still of importance to researchers and professionals, either for the source material they contain, or as landmarks in the history of their academic discipline.

Drawing from the world-renowned collections in the Cambridge University Library, and guided by the advice of experts in each subject area, Cambridge University Press is using state-of-the-art scanning machines in its own Printing House to capture the content of each book selected for inclusion. The files are processed to give a consistently clear, crisp image, and the books finished to the high quality standard for which the Press is recognised around the world. The latest print-on-demand technology ensures that the books will remain available indefinitely, and that orders for single or multiple copies can quickly be supplied.

The Cambridge Library Collection brings back to life books of enduring scholarly value (including out-of-copyright works originally issued by other publishers) across a wide range of disciplines in the humanities and social sciences and in science and technology.

The Magical Ritual of the Sanctum Regnum

Interpreted by the Tarot Trumps

ÉLIPHAS LÉVI
EDITED AND TRANSLATED BY
W. WYNN WESTCOTT

CAMBRIDGE
UNIVERSITY PRESS

CAMBRIDGE UNIVERSITY PRESS

Cambridge, New York, Melbourne, Madrid, Cape Town,
Singapore, São Paolo, Delhi, Tokyo, Mexico City

Published in the United States of America by Cambridge University Press, New York

www.cambridge.org
Information on this title: www.cambridge.org/9781108044295

© in this compilation Cambridge University Press 2012

This edition first published 1896
This digitally printed version 2012

ISBN 978-1-108-04429-5 Paperback

This book reproduces the text of the original edition. The content and language reflect
the beliefs, practices and terminology of their time, and have not been updated.

Cambridge University Press wishes to make clear that the book, unless originally published
by Cambridge, is not being republished by, in association or collaboration with, or
with the endorsement or approval of, the original publisher or its successors in title.

The original edition of this book contains a number of colour plates,
which have been reproduced in black and white. Colour versions of these
images can be found online at www.cambridge.org/9781108044295

THE MAGICAL RITUAL

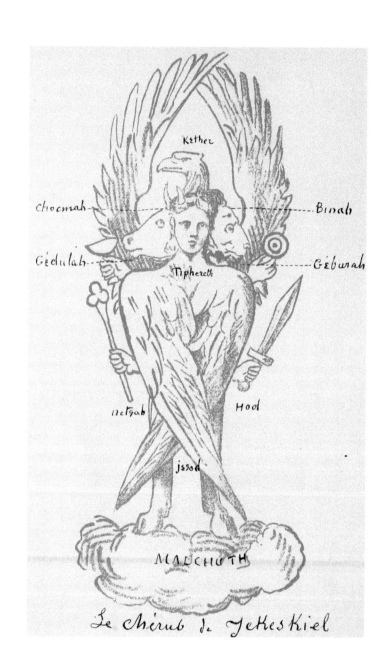

Kether

Chocmah

Binah

Gédulah

Géburah

Tiphereth

Netzah

Hod

Jésod

MALCHUTH

Le Chérub de Jéheskiel

THE MAGICAL RITUAL

OF THE

SANCTUM REGNUM

INTERPRETED BY THE

TAROT TRUMPS

TRANSLATED FROM THE MSS. OF

ÉLIPHAZ LÉVI

AND EDITED BY

W. WYNN WESTCOTT, M.B.

MAGUS OF THE ROSICRUCIAN SOCIETY OF ENGLAND

WITH EIGHT PLATES

LONDON

GEORGE REDWAY

1896

PREFACE BY THE EDITOR

THIS translation of a previously unpublished work by the late Alphonse Louis Constant, or, as he preferred to call himself, Éliphaz Lévi, is published with the consent of its possessor, Mr. Edward Maitland, the eminent collaborateur of the late Dr. Anna Kingsford, to whom it was given by the Baron Spedalieri, so well known as the friend, disciple, and literary heir of Éliphaz Lévi. The original MSS., which is in the handwriting of Lévi himself, is written upon pages interleaved with the text of a printed copy of a work by Trithemius of Spanheim, entitled *De Septem Secundeis:* the edition was published at Cologne, and is dated 1567. This work of the Abbot Trithemius is a very curious and interesting dissertation upon the ruling of the world by the seven great Archangels, to each of whom in succession is allotted a period of 354 years and 4 months. The Archangels are referred to the Planets

of the ancients, and their successive periods of
dominion are taken in the following order :—

Orifiel	representing	Saturn
Anael	,,	Venus
Zachariel	,,	Jupiter
Raphael	,,	Mercury
Samael	,,	Mars
Gabriel	,,	Luna
Michael	,,	Sol

The first course of these rulers ended in Anno Mundi
2480. The Noachian Deluge is placed at 1656, in
the reign of Samael. The destruction of the Tower
of Babel (see Tarot Trump, No. XVI., page 63)
occurred in the Second reign of Orifiel; the life of
Abraham in the Second reign of Zachariel; the life
of Moses in the Second reign of Raphael; Pythagoras,
Xerxes, and Alexander the Great in the Second
Solar reign of Michael.

The era of Jesus Christ comes in the Third reign
of Orifiel.

The Third reign of Anael	began in	109, A.D.
,, ,, ,, Zachariel	,,	463
,, ,, ,, Raphael	,,	817
,, ,, ,, Samael	,,	1171
,, ,, ,, Gabriel	,,	1525
,, ,, ,, Michael	,,	1879

Lévi appears to have been deeply impressed with

this system of Rule by Archangels, and Edward Maitland, in his life of Dr. Anna Kingsford, refers to this volume with approval.

Under the heading of "Notes" the editor has given a short description of each Tarot Trump at the end of each chapter, and also a few notes on the mystical meanings assigned to the Tarots by Éliphaz Lévi in his other works ; some of the views of P. Christian are added. To facilitate reference to such information, a table is added here specifying the places to which the student can turn for further opinions and more detailed descriptions.

Court de Gebelin. Le Monde premitif analysé. Paris. 1773–82. Volume 8.

Etteilla or Alliette. Philosophie des hautes sciences. Amsterdam. 1785.

Etteilla. Leçons theoriques et pratiques du livre du Thot. 1787.

Tarots Egyptiennes ou Grand Etteilla. 1830.

Etteila. Manière de se récreer avec le jeu des Tarots. 1783–5.

Lévi, Éliphaz. *Nom de plume* of Alphonse Louis Constant.

Rituel de la Haute Magie. Paris. 1861. Pages 344–356 give the several descriptions and meanings of the Tarot Trumps; but the whole chapter entitled "Le livre d'Hermes," pages 332–384, is concerned with the subject. These Trumps are also allotted to Lunar days at pages 265-269.

Dogme de la Haute Magie. Paris. 1861. The tenth chapter has especial reference to the Tarot; but the whole volume is divided into chapters which relate to the Trumps.

Histoire de la Magie. 1860. Refer to pages 46, 81, and 109.

P. Christian. Histoire de la Magie. Paris. Special descriptions and occult meanings of the Tarot Trumps are given on pages 114-131.

Papus. Le Tarot des Bohemiens. English translation by Morton. George Redway. 1896.

Wirth, Oswald. Le livre de Thot.

Waite, A. E. The Mysteries of Magic, a Digest of the Writings of Éliphaz Lévi. London. George Redway. 1886. See pages 242-265.

MacGregor Mathers, S. L. The Tarot, its Occult Significance. George Redway. 1888.

Willshire, W. H. A Descriptive Catalogue of Playing and other Cards in the British Museum. 1876.

Chatto, W. A. Facts and Speculations on the Origin and History of Playing Cards. 1848.

The ordinary reader who has made no special study of the magical writings of Éliphaz Lévi, nor of the Kabalah, may consider that, however interesting the subject-matter of many of the following chapters, the connection between the Tarot Trumps and the details given under each heading is but slight. It must be understood that there *is* in all cases a direct relation between card and subject; but the keys which connect them are missing by intention of the author, and yet are obtainable by study of Lévi's other works.

The twenty-two Tarot Trumps bear a relation to numbers and to letters; the true attributions are known, so far as is ascertainable, to but a few students, members of the Hermetic schools: the attributions given by Lévi in his *Dogme* and *Rituel*, by Christian, and by Papus are incorrect, presumably by design. The editor has seen a manuscript page of cypher about 150 years old which has a different attribution, and one which has been found by several occult students, well known to him, to satisfy all the conditions required by occult science.

The eight coloured plates with which this volume is embellished are facsimile copies of Lévi's own drawings; they add greatly to the charm of the work, and are a credit to the publisher and to the artist who executed them. The design on the cover is the monogram drawn by Lévi to represent the "Completion of the Great Work," see page 45. The Cross — four, multiplied by the triangle — three, gives twelve the complete number of a cycle: the Hebrew letter Tau represents the Universe.

" The Mysteries of Magic, a Digest of the Writings of Éliphaz Lévi," by Mr. A. E. Waite, published by Mr. Redway in 1886, has had so large a circulation among English readers, that the editor anticipates a cordial reception for this little volume.

LONDON, *February* 1896.

THE MAGICAL RITUAL OF THE SANCTUM REGNUM

I

THE MAGICIAN—LE BATELEUR

LISTEN to the words of Solomon which he spake to his
son Rehoboam: "The fear of God is the beginning
of wisdom, but the end of wisdom is the knowledge
and love of Him who is the Source of all good, and
the supreme Reason, whence all things do proceed."
Adonai had passed an eternity in heaven, and then
created Man; so a time on earth is given to man to
comprehend Adonai. In other words, the knowledge
which man attains concerning the Supreme Being
springs from the faculties which have been bestowed
upon him at his creation, in order that he might in
his turn formulate an image of the Being who has
sent him into this world.

A

By Intelligence man conceives the ideal of God, and by Will he should turn to good works. But human will when without works is dead, or at any rate is only a vague desire : the same is true of a thought not expressed in language; it is not a word, but only a dream of the intelligence. An imagination is not a realised thing, it is only a promised something, while an act is a reality. For the same reason there is no piety without prayer, and no religion without worship. Words are the formal and social reality of ideals, and ceremonies are religion put into practice; there is no real faith unless it shows itself by actions prompted by faith. A formulated expression in words, confirmed by actions, demonstrates the two powers of a human soul. To work it is necessary to will, and to will it is necessary to formulate the desire. Actions imply ideas even if the ideals are not themselves translated into acts.

Thought is the life of intelligence, words show the creative force of thought, while actions are the last effort of words, and the desirable complement of words. Words have been spoken, thought has been translated into action; by the act of creating, speech has taken place.

A word is the requisite formula of a thought, an act is an exhibition of will. This is why prayer is a necessity, and may obtain all that it asks. A prayer is a perfected act of the will, it is a link connecting human words with the divine Will. All ceremonies consecrations, ablutions, and sacrifices are prayers in action, and are symbolic formulas; and they are the most potent prayers because they are translations of word into action, showing will power and persistence, seeing that they require more constrained attention than silent prayer, or prayer expressed in words; and so they constitute real work, and such work demands a man's whole energy.

Notes.

The First Tarot Trump is named Le Bateleur, and in English is spoken of as the Magician. Lévi remarks in one of his works that the arms and body of the figure bear a resemblance to the first letter, Aleph, of the Hebrew alphabet, in some packs of the oldest designs; but the student will do wisely to consult his intuition, if he have no adept instructor, as to the true attribution of this or either of the other trumps of the Tarot.

The Magician stands by a table holding a magical wand in his left hand; before him on the table are lying other implements suitable to his task, such as a dagger, cup, and pantacle. His face expresses assurance, and intelligence beams from his eyes.

Lévi elsewhere defines its occult meaning to be God, spirit, unity; and man as a reflection of God. P. Christian, in his *Histoire de la Magie*, says that this card represents, in the Divine world, the Absolute One; in the Intellectual world, Unity; and in the Physical world, Man; and that man should, like God, work without ceasing, for a state of willing nothing and doing nothing is hardly less fatal than evil doing.

II

THE PRIESTESS—LA PAPESSE

DEPTH is equal to height, darkness is contrasted
with light, matter is but the garment of the spirit.
That which is below is like that which is above.
The breath of God is borne along over the waters,
and the waters remain aloft carried on by the breath
of God. That which we call the Breath of God is
the Life Essence spread over the worlds; it is that
warm luminous fluid which gives a soul to the
planets; the common reservoir of progressive animal
life; the universal basis of the sympathies between
bodies, and the medium of love between souls; it is
the vehicle of the will, and common basis for all the
varied modifications of the Creative Word. The Breath
of the mouth of God leads to the corresponding
human breath. God said, "Let us make man," and
man answers, "Let us make to ourselves a God."

When God made creation manifest as a temple,
He illumined the planets as light-bearers, He decorated the earth with flowers as an altar, He gave
mysterious properties to metals and plants, and He

drew with His finger circles, triangles, and the cross, as eternal pantacles, traced in living fire upon the immense vault of the skies. The Magus should imitate his God upon this earth, his dwelling.

Know, Will, and Act; these are the three essentials for sacerdotal and royal high magic. Matter and form are instruments placed in the power of the Magus, his acts should be dependent on the Word, and so shall none of his deeds be lost, and his teachings shall be preserved.

You then who desire to understand the mysteries of this Science and to perform marvels, consider and tremble lest you have as yet failed to attain to knowledge and wisdom; for if so, you stand on the brink of an abyss; stop, ere it is too late. But if you have secured the Lamp and Wand of Initiation, if you are cognisant of the secrets of the Nine, if you never speak of God without the Light which proceeds from Him, if you have received the mystical baptism of the Four Elements, if you have prayed upon the Seven Mountains, if you know the mode of motion of the Double Sphynxed Chariot, if you have grasped the dogma of why Osiris was a black god, if you are free, if you are a king, if you are in truth a priest in the temple of Solomon—act without fear, and speak, for your words will be all-powerful in the spiritual kingdom, and the breath of God will follow the utterances of your mouth, and the powers of the heavens and of the earth will be obedient unto you.

Notes.

The Second Tarot Trump represents a seated female figure, crowned with a tiara, and holding a book in her hands; it is partly concealed by her mantle. She has a veil around her head, and some old cards show the horns of Isis upon her head-dress. Some authors who discredit the great age and Egyptian origin of the Tarot symbols have asserted that this card was intended to represent the fabulous Pope Joan. This character was said to be an Englishwoman of great learning, ability, and vice, who was chosen Pope in A.D. 855, succeeding Leo IV. Both Protestants and Roman Catholics have now rejected the story as a groundless fiction. Lévi, in his *Dogme de la haute Magie*, throws out the suggestion that this trump represents the Greek Juno, and he assigns as its occult meanings— the house of God, and of man; sanctuary, the Gnosis, the Kabalah, the dyad, woman and maternity.

The Rosicrucians considered this card to be Isis, the Great Mother, Soul of Nature. P. Christian gives as its meaning—Occult Science awaiting the initiate at the door of the sanctuary.

III

THE EMPRESS—L'IMPERATRICE

You should before all other things study and understand the sacred laws of Nature. Discern the Father Spirit and Mother Spirit, and recognise the sex aspect of the two breaths, and the soul of their movements; learn how the black female seeks the caresses of the white male, and why the white male does not disdain the dark woman. The white man is Day, or the Sun; and the black woman refers to Night, and the Moon. It is necessary to know the names and powers of the twelve precious jewels which are included in the crown of gold referred to the Sun, and the names also which are allotted to the chief of the powers of the Moon. You will then require to be familiar with the keys of the Fifty Gates, the secret of the Thirty-two Paths, and the characters of the Seven Spirits.

These Seven Spirits are, Michael of the Sun, Gabriel of the Moon, Samael of Mars, Raphael of Mercury, Zachariel of Jupiter, Anael of Venus, and Orifiel of

Saturn. These govern the world in successive order, and the completion of their seven ages of ruling power constitutes a Week of the Time of God.

You must learn also the plants, colours, perfumes, and musical notes which correspond to the seven planetary powers; and it is essential to retain those correspondences with the utmost exactitude. Thus when it is required to do perfect magical work, the procedure of each day is different in many particulars.

On Sunday you must wear a purple robe, a tiara, and golden bracelets; you must arrange about the altar or tripod, garlands of laurel, heliotrope, or sunflower; you must use as a fumigating incense cinnamon, frankincense, saffron, and red sandal-wood; you require at your right hand a golden wand set with a ruby or a chrysolite; and your operations must be carried out between one hour past midnight up to eight in the morning, or between three in the afternoon and ten in the evening.

On Monday you should wear a white robe with silver ornaments, with a collar of three rows consisting of pearls, crystals, and selenites; a tiara yellow with the letters of Gabriel in silver. The proper perfumes are those of camphor, white sandal-wood, amber, and cucumber seeds; the garlands for the altar should be of armoise (*query*, mugwort, artemisia), evening primrose, and yellow ranunculus. Avoid with care anything of black colour; use no cup or vessel of gold, silver only, or clear white china or pottery. The same hours as before mentioned for the Sun, but use rather the night hours.

On Tuesday the colour of the robe should be fiery, or rusty, or of blood colour, with a girdle and bracelets of steel; the wand should be of magnetised steel; a sword may also be used and a consecrated dagger; garlands of absinth and rue; an amethyst and steel ring on the finger should also be worn.

On Wednesday the robe should be green or of shot silk many tinted; the necklet of pearls, or of glass beads containing mercury; the perfumes are benzoin, myrrh, and storax; the flowers for the garlands are the narcissus, lily, the annual or perennial mercurialis, fumitory, or marjoram; the precious stone is the agate.

On Thursday the robe of scarlet, a lamen of tin upon the forehead, bearing the symbol of Jupiter and the three words Giazar of Fire, Bethor of Water, and Samgabiel, also fiery; the perfumes for incense, ambergris, cardamon, grains of paradise, balm, mace, and saffron. The ring should contain an emerald or a sapphire; the garlands of oak, poplar, fig-tree, or pomegranate; the wand of glass or resin. The robe should be made of wool or silk.

On Friday the robe of azure blue, its decorations of green or rose colour, the wand of polished copper; the perfumes are musk, civet, and amber; crown of violets; garlands of roses interspersed with boughs of myrtle and olive; the ring ornamented by a turquoise. Lapis lazuli and beryl should decorate the crown or diadem. The operator should hold a fan formed of swan's feathers, and should wear around his loins a circlet, being a copper plate on which is engraved Anael, with its sigil, and on a circle surrounding these the words Ave Evah; Vade Lilith.

On Saturday the robe should be black, or dark brown, with appropriate designs embroidered in orange-coloured silk. Around the neck should be worn a chain and lamen formed of lead engraved with the name Saturn and his sigil, with the addition of the words Almalec, Aphiel, and Zarahiel. The proper perfumes for the incense are scammony, aloes, sulphur, and asafœtida. The wand should be ornamented with an onyx stone, and the proper garlands are of ash, cyprus, and black hellebore. Upon the onyx on the wand there should be engraved with a consecrated tool, during the hours of Saturn, a figure of the double-faced Janus.

NOTES.

The Third Tarot Trump, the Empress, represents a seated female figure upon a throne, crowned with twelve stars, and holding in her left hand a sceptre surmounted by a diamond-shaped emblem, or a globe; she has wings, and by her right side is emblazoned on a shield the black eagle. This figure is the Greek Aphrodite-Urania, and corresponds to the figure in St. John's vision, clothed with the Sun, crowned with twelve stars, and having the Moon beneath her feet.

Lévi gives in his *Rituel* its meanings as the Word, the ternary, plenitude, fecundity, nature. See also Waite, page 255. Christian, page 116, allots Isis to this trump. This is erroneous; no examples of the Empress ever show horns, while several Priestess cards of the oldest types do show the horns of Isis upon her head.

IV

THE EMPEROR—L'EMPEREUR

THE clothing of a Magician should be new, clean, and woven by a virgin; magical implements should be new, and consecrated by prayers and incense.

The Magician needs to be abstinent, chaste, and devoted to the Work. His spirit and heart must be free from other claims upon them, and his will power devoted wholly, perseveringly, and with intelligent faith to the success of any great work, and to the results of his scientific occult performances. Magical operations should commence with Exorcisms of air, earth, and water, and end by Consecrations with fire.

The Exorcism of Air is performed by breathing forth toward the four cardinal points, by the Word, and by repeating this invocation :—

"The Spirit of God brooded over the waters, and God breathed into Man the breath of life.

"The Spirit of God filled the universe; in it all things exist, and in it is the Word of Power.

"May the Word be in my spirit, and so may all things be subservient to me.

"Be ye exorcised then, ye beings of Air, in the Name of Him whose breath first filled all things with the Holy Spirit.   Amen."

The Prayer of the Sylphs should then be recited.

[This will be found at length in Lévi's *Rituel de la haute Magie*, p. 78, and in English in A. E. Waite's "Mysteries of Magic," p. 122, the only error being his heading, "Prayer *for* the Sylphs"; it is the prayer *of* the Sylphs for a nearer relation to the divinity.]

The Exorcism of Earth is performed by the sprinkling of consecrated water, by the breath, by the Word, and by the burning of incense suitable to the day of the ceremony.   Then recite the Prayer of the Gnomes.

[See Lévi, *Rituel*, p. 84; and Waite, p. 125.]

The Exorcism of Water is performed by the laying on of hands, by the breath, by the Word, and by sprinkling upon it consecrated salt mixed with a little of the ash taken from the censer, and duly consecrated.   The Water is to be sprinkled around by a brush composed of sprays of vervain, periwinkle, sage, mint, valerian, and basil; these are to be tied with a thread taken from a virgin's distaff, to a handle of the wood of a nut-tree which has not yet borne fruit. Upon this handle you must engrave, with the magical dagger, the characters of the Seven Spirits.

The Salt is consecrated by reciting over it the following Latin prayer :—

" In isto Sale sit sapientia, et ab omni corruptione servet mentes nostras et corpora nostra, per Chokmah, et in virtute Ruach Chokmael; recedant ab isto phantasmata hylæ ut sit Sal celestis, Sal terræ et Terra salis, ut nutrietur bos triturans, et addat spei nostræ cornua tauri volantis. Amen."

Then this Latin prayer over the ashes from the censer :—

" Revertatur cinis ad fontem aquarum viventium, et fiat terra fructificans et germinat arborem jucunditatis, et incensum suavitatis, per tria nomina Binah, Chokmah et Kether, in principio et in fine, per Alpha et Omega, qui sunt in Spiritu Azoth. Amen."

While you sprinkle the mixed salt and ashes into the water, recite :—

"Emittes Spiritum O Tiphereth, et creabuntur omnia nova in his ergo sit semen venturi sæculi. Amen."

EXORCISM OF WATER.

" All powerful Father, God of Abraham, Isaac, and Jacob, whose voice is heard in the great waters, who

didst cleave the waters of the Red Sea to make a
passage for the children of Israel, and then didst
cause the sea to swallow up the Egyptians who were
pursuing them, Mi Kamoka Baalim Jehovah, thou
whose altar, composed of the Twelve Jewels, is beneath the waters of the sacred river, deign to bless
this water and to banish from it all baneful influences,
Shaddai, Shaddai, Shaddai (breathe three times over
the water).   By the great names, Araritha, Eloah va
Daath, Elohim Tzabaoth and Elohim Gibur, may this
water be consecrated for the service of those who are
about to invoke the Divine Powers for the benefit of
their souls.   Amen."

Then the Prayer of the Undines should be recited.
[This is found in the *Rituel*, p. 81, and in Waite,
p. 123.]

To perform the Exorcism of Fire, cast upon it salt,
incense, and sulphur, while you pronounce the names
of Anael, Michael, and Samael; the prayer of the
Salamanders should then be recited.

[This is to be found in the *Rituel*, p. 83, and in
Waite, p. 124.]

You must thoroughly understand that elemental
beings are souls of an imperfect type, not yet raised
in the scale up to human existence, and that they
can only manifest power when called into action by

the adept as auxiliaries to his will, by means of that universal astral fluid in which they live. The kingdom of the Gnomes is assigned to the North, the Salamanders to the South, the Sylphs to the East, and the Undines to the West.

These Elemental beings are related to, and bear an influence over persons, according as they are of one or other of the four Temperaments. The Gnomes are related to the Melancholic type, Salamanders to the Sanguine, Undines to the Phlegmatic, and Sylphs to the Bilious Temperament.

Their symbols are those of Taurus the Bull for Gnomes; Leo the Lion for Salamanders; the Eagle for Sylphs; and the sign of Aquarius for Undines.

Their Rulers are respectively Ghob, Djin, Paralda, and Nicsa.

The combination of these four types of face and being represents the Created Universe, a complete and eternal entity, Man in fact, the Microcosm; and this is the first formula of the mystical explanation of the enigma of the Sphynx.

NOTES.

The Fourth Tarot Trump represents a crowned emperor reclining against a throne, holding a sceptre in his right hand; the sceptre ends above in a lotus flower. In modern tarots the throne is decorated with a black eagle. The older design showed the emperor's body as representing a right-angled triangle in general outline, and the legs are crossed, the whole suggesting the Athanor of the Alchemist. Lévi, in his *Rituel*, gives the following meanings to this card : The Porte, or government of the Orientals, initiation, power, the Tetragrammaton, quaternary, and the cubical stone.

Christian considers that on the human plane this trump means the realisation of actions directed by the science of truth, the love of justice, the force of will, and organic work.

THE PENTAGRAM.

Seal of the Microcosm.

V

THE POPE, OR HIEROPHANT—LE PAPE

To control the Will power and make it subservient
to the law of Intelligence—this is the Great Work
of our sacerdotal art. Ceremonies are made use
of to educate the Will by means of the Imagination. Ceremonies which are performed without
intelligence and without faith; in the absence of
the higher aspirations of the soul, are but superstitious observances which tend to degrade those
who take part in them. It is an error to attribute
Magical Power to ceremonials, for Magical Power
exists only in the trained Will of the operator. For
this reason is the Magical Axiom true, that the
Sanctum Regnum—the Divine Kingdom—the Kingdom of God—is *within* us. I.N.R.I., Intra nobis
Regnum DeI; and hence also is it that great
marvels can be shown by the PENTAGRAM, which
is the seal of the Microcosm; for the Microcosm is
the reflection of the Macrocosm; the Microcosm
is Man and his human Will; he is the reflection of

the Universe, which is the Macrocosm. The Man whose Intelligence has received culture can by his Will Power, exerted through the Pentagram, control and command the powers and beings of the Elements, and restrain evil elementaries from their perverse works.

The HEXAGRAM is the symbol of the Macrocosm; it is often called the Seal of Solomon. It consists of two interlaced triangles; the erect triangle is of flame colour, the inverse triangle is coloured blue. In the centre space there may be drawn a Tau Cross and three Hebrew Yods, or a Crux ansata, or the Triple Tau of the Arch-masons. He who with Intelligence and Will is armed with this emblem has need of no other thing, he should be all potent, for this is the perfect sign of the Absolute.

This is the Monogram of Hermetic Truth; it expresses the subject of the Great Work. It is made up of Hebrew, Greek, and Latin letters, and the mode of expressing this ideal in the presence of un-initiates is by the word Azoth, or by the name Magnēs: other Magi have applied to it the titles of the flying dragon of Medea, and the serpent of the mystical Eden.

THE HEXAGRAM.

Symbol of the Macrocosm.

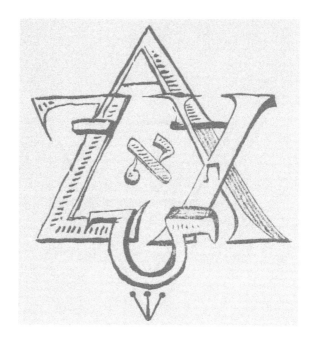

A Z O T H.

Monogram of Hermetic Truth.

See Page 20.

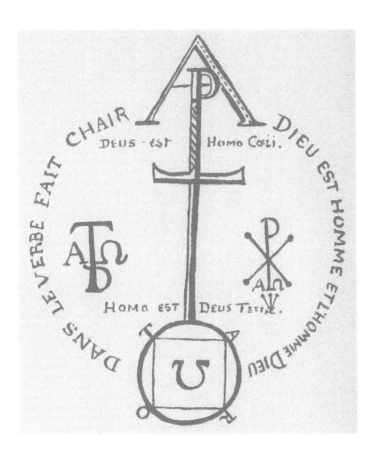

A Monogram of the

GNOSIS.

See Page 21.

THE TETRAGRAM,

traced in a Kabalistic design.

See Page 21.

This is the high and incommunicable TETRAGRAM traced in a Kabalistic and Hermetic design. All initiates, even of the first grade, will at once understand its symbolism.

This emblem is the monogram of the Universal Gnosis; it is formed of Greek and Latin letters; it expresses by symbols the secrets of the Wheel of Ezekiel, and the Book of St. John the Evangelist; it includes the sign of the Labarum of Constantine.

This emblem naturally shows the word ROTA; but viewed in the light of the Kalabah, the word TAROT.

These Characters, with the Philosophic Cross, include all science *in esse*, and those who are initiates of the Grand Arcanum need no further symbols or emblems; nor do those adepts who know the true but concealed meanings and powers of the words JAKIN and BOAZ, which are related to the two Pillars at the Porch of the Temple, one of which was of white marble, and the other of black, while both were decorated with Brazen ornaments. By these Characters the spirits of evil nature are bound and held in control; by these also, if the operator be just and pure, he makes himself known to angels and may incline them to his aims. For indeed nothing can resist in magical arts the combined powers of the Pentagram, Hexagram, and Tetragram divine.

All other signs, seals, and symbols are but arbitrary, and the keys of their meaning may be found in the Steganographia, or the Polygraphia of, the Abbot Trithemius of Spanheim, or else in the magical treatises of Peter of Abano, of Paracelsus, of Arbatel, or of Cornelius Agrippa.

Notes.

The Tarot Trump numbered 5, named the Pope, Hierophant, or Jupiter, represents a crowned ruler bearing a tripled cross wand in his left hand : he is seated between two pillars. The meanings assigned by El. Lévi are—religion, philosophy, symbolism, law, instruction, and demonstration. The right hand of the Pope gives the sign of occult wisdom, and not the usual papal benediction.

P. Christian decides that this card shows in the Divine World, Universal Law; in the Intellectual World, Religion; and in the Physical World, such inspiration as is communicated by the Astral fluidic force.

VI

THE LOVERS—L'AMOUREUX

EVER bear in mind that Equilibrium results only from the opposition of forces; the active has no existence without the passive; light without darkness produces no form; and affirmation can only triumph over negation. Love again gains accession of strength from hate, and that hell is the heated soil of such plants as shall bear root in heaven. It should be known also that the great Fluidic Agent which is called the "Soul of the World," and which is delineated with the horned head of the Cow of Isis to express animal fecundity, is a blind force.

The power which the Magus wields is composed of two opposing forces, which unite in love and disjoin in discord; love associates contraries, while hate makes similars to be rivals and enemies; hatred succeeds to love when by saturation the void has become filled, unless the full cannot become empty;

but the usual result is an equilibrated saturation, due to mutual repulsions.

From these considerations can be deduced the existence and causes of sympathy and antipathy between persons, and so the means of becoming loved can be shown to those who are good as well as wise and discreet.

Sexual love is a physical manifestation; repugnance and pain may be forgotten by those who are under its sway. This is a form of inebriation arising from the attraction of two contrary fluids; and at the conjunction of the positive and negative poles there results an ecstasy and orgasm during which the loved one seems the brilliant phantom of a vision.

When the conjunction has set up the state of equilibrium anew, attraction is succeeded by repulsion; and very often an exaggerated amour leads to an unjust share of disgust.

All created beings participate either in the positive or negative attitude of the universal sympathetic fluid, and may help to maintain or re-establish a Sympathy; but it is necessary to distrust knowledge while it is imperfect, and not to expose oneself in suggesting remedies to the risk of administering poisons. Enchantment by means of any object which has belonged to a beloved one is often a magnetic operation leading to useless and yet dangerous results; it is better to establish new currents of force, to produce a void where satiety exists, for the surest means of regaining the affection of man or woman is to bestow some signs of love on another.

Consider the bodily and mental disorders which result from solitude and its accompanying fluidic congestions, due to want of equilibrium;—such are nervous maladies, hysteria, hypochondriasis, megrim, vapours, and insane delusions. It will be possible also to understand the ailments of maidens, and of women of an uncertain age, of widows and of celibates. Inspired by the natural law now under consideration, you may often predict the future course of a life, and may cure many such ailments, often by distracting the attention when unduly fixed, and so may the Magus become as great a physician as Paracelsus, or as renowned a Diviner as was Cornelius Agrippa. You will come to understand the diseases of the soul; the fact that learned and chaste persons often hunger after the pleasures of vice will be noticed, and so will it be observed that men and women steeped in vices turn at times to the consolations of virtue; and thus you may predict, without striking a blow, the occurrence of strange conversions and of unexpected sins, and great astonishment will be shown at your facility in discerning the most carefully concealed secrets of the heart and home. Girls and women may be by such means of divination shown in dreams the forms of lover and husband; such confidantes are potent auxiliaries in magic arts; never abuse their position, never neglect their interests, for they are good gifts to the Magus. In order to possess an assured sway over the heads and hearts of women, it is essential to obtain the favour of both Gabriel the Angel of the Moon, and of Anäel the Angel of Venus.

Certain female evil demons must be overcome and cast down; foremost of these are :—

Nahémah, princess of the Succubi of the dreams of men.

Lilith, queen of the Stryges, tempting to debauchery, and destroyer of maternal desire.

Nahémah presides also over illicit and sterile caresses.

Lilith rejoices in strangling in their cradles children whose origin has been soiled by the touch of Nahémah.

The truly wise master of the Kabalah understands the concealed meaning of these names, and of such demoniac evil powers, which are also called the material envelopes or cortices, or shells of the Tree of Life, soiled and blackened by the outer darkness; they are as branches which are dead, having been torn off from the Tree, whence issue light, life, and love.

NOTES.

The Tarot Trump numbered 6, which is named in French packs L'Amoureux, is commonly called in this country The Lovers. The design shows the Sun above, whence issues Cupid armed with a bow and arrow; below is a man standing between two women, who represent Virtue and Vice. The meanings assigned by Él. Lévi are—equilibrium, antagonism, union, interlacement, the conflict of two triads.

P. Christian says : " In the Divine World this card teaches the knowledge of good and evil; in the Intellectual World, the equilibrium of necessity and liberty; and in the Physical World, the relation of cause and effect.

VII

THE CHARIOT OF HERMES—LE CHARIOT

THE Chariot of Hermes has attached to its car a white and also a black Sphynx; each of these symbolic animals propounds an enigma to the neophyte. The word of the White Sphynx is Jachin. The word of the Black Sphynx is Boaz. The former word here signifies Love; the latter word here signifies Power. Samael guides the White Sphynx, Anael guides the Black Sphynx; because attraction is set up by contraries. Hermes, seated in the Chariot, touches the Black Sphynx with the point of a sword of steel, but the White Sphynx with a sceptre of gold.

It is after the type founded by the Thrice Great Hermes that the Magus learns how to use the Magical Wand and the Sword to control good and evil powers and beings.

Evil beings fear the sword because their astral forms are subject to wounds and to being severed by such a weapon. White spirits obey tho consecrated

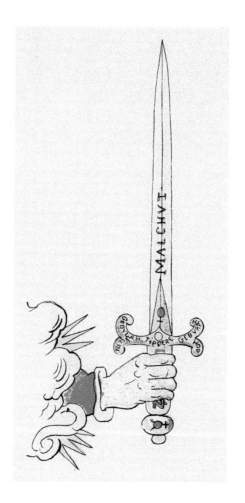

THE   MAGICAL   SWORD.

magical wand because of its correspondence to the
type of the Wand of the God-sent magician Moses.

FORMATION AND CONSECRATION OF A MAGICAL SWORD.

The sword-blade of steel should be forged in the
hour of Mars, and new smith's tools should be used.
The pommel should be of silver, made hollow, and containing a little quicksilver; the symbols of Mercury
and Luna, with the monograms of Gabriel and Samael,
should be engraved upon its surface. The hilt should be
encased with tin, and should have the symbol of Jupiter
and the monogram of Michael engraved upon it; see
Cornelius Agrippa, *De occulta Philosophia*, liber iii.,
cap. 30. There should be a small triangular copper
plate extending from the hilt up the blade of the
sword a short distance on each side; on these should
be engraved the symbols of Venus and Mercury.

The guard should end in two curved plates on each
side; on these, the words Gedulah, Netzach upon one
side, and Geburah, Hod upon the other, should be
engraved; and in the middle between them engrave
the Sephirotic name, Tiphereth.

Upon the blade itself engrave upon one side Malkuth, and upon the other side the words *Quis ut
Deus*.

The Consecration of the Magical Sword must be performed on a Sunday during the Solar hour and under the invoked power of Michael. Drape the Altar, prepare the Tripod, and burn therein the wood of laurel and cypress, consecrate the fire, and then thrust the blade of the sword into it, saying, " Elohim Tzabaoth, by the power of the Tetragrammaton, in the name of Adonai and of Mikael, may this sword become a weapon of might to scatter the beings of the unseen world, may its use in war bring peace, may it be brilliant as Tiphereth, terrible as Geburah, and merciful as Chesed." Withdraw the sword from the fire, and quench it in a liquid composed of the blood of a reptile mixed with the sap to be obtained from a green laurel : then polish the blade with the ashes of vervain carefully burned.

FORMATION AND CONSECRATION OF THE MAGIC WAND.

Choose the wood of an almond or nut tree which has just flowered for the first time ; the bough should be cut off at one blow by the magical sickle. It must be bored evenly from end to end without any crack or injury, and a magnetised steel needle of the same length must be introduced. One end must be closed by a clear transparent glass bead, and the other end by a similar bead of resin : cover up these two ends with sachets of silk. Fit two rings near the middle of the wand, one of copper and one of zinc, and supply two portions of fine chain of the same metals; roll them round the wand, and fix the ends into the wand close to the ends. Upon the wand should then be written the names of the Twelve Spirits of the Zodiacal Cycle; their sigils should also be added.

Aries	Sarahiel
Taurus	Araziel
Gemini	Saraiel
Cancer	Phakiel
Leo	Seratiel
Virgo	Schaltiel
Libra	Chadakiel
Scorpio	Sartziel
Sagittarius	Saritiel
Capricornus	Semaqiel
Aquarius	Tzakmaqiel
Pisces	Vacabiel

Upon the Copper Ring engrave in Hebrew letters from right to left the words " The Holy Jerusalem," H QDSнH JRUSнLIM ; and upon the Zinc Ring engrave in Hebrew letters from right to left the words " The King Solomon," H MLK SнLMH, Heh Melek Shelomoh.

When the wand is complete, it must be consecrated by invocations of spirits of the Four Elements and the Seven Planets by ceremonies lasting over the seven days of a week, using the special incense and prayers as already described for each day.

The consecrated Wand, and indeed all magical implements, should be kept wrapped in silk, and never allowed in contact with any colour but black; and it is well to keep them in a cedar or ebony box.

With this Wand duly made and fully consecrated, the Magus can cure unknown diseases, he may enchant a person, or cause him to fall asleep at will, can wield the forces of the elements and cause the oracles to speak.

Notes.

In this chapter Lévi describes the Tarot Trump No. 7, the Chariot; in his *Rituel* he assigns its meanings, as — Weapon, sword, sacred septenary, triumph, royalty, priesthood.

In respect to this card P. Christian writes that in the Divine World it refers to the dominance of spirit over natural force; in the Intellectual World, Priesthood and authority; in the Physical World, the submission of matter to the intelligence and will-power of man.

This seventh key is figured in Lévi's *Rituel* in a full-paged plate facing page 332.

VIII

JUSTICE—LA JUSTICE

You must never forget that the priest is a king, and
the wise man is a judge. There are in this world
both the weak and the strong, the poor and the rich,
there are both the ignorant and the learned. The
former are ever the servitors of the latter; but if the
former do their works worthily they thereby become
worthy of admission to the concourse of masters,
while the useless servants are to be cast away. It
is well, therefore, to teach men how to serve well, so
that they may come forward into a place of power.
All things upon this world, and all below the surface,
belong to the domain of man.

Created beings roar, groan, hiss, coo, and weave
around man as a centre; man alone speaks to his
fellows and to God ; and the voice of God upon earth
is spoken through man. The science of life is written
in the Book of Nature, but man alone can read it.
The wise and powerful translate the words of this

C

book into creeds and symbols for the instruction of
the feeble and ignorant. When you speak to such
as are like children, speak as to children. Do not
sell the secrets of wisdom, and do not divulge them
to pander to curiosity.

A man should form his opinions in freedom, and
thus he may resemble the ideal of divinity. Cast
not the pearls of mystic science before those of low
and evil mind who have no knowledge, those whom
the Testament calls swine. To such persons, whether
you speak the truth, or veil the truth, there is but
misunderstanding; deception haunts them, they esti-
mate all things by a faulty conscience. You may
dazzle them by the glancing of the sword, but do not
let them approach the wand or clavicule. If you
wish to have no need to fear an evil person, make
him fear you. Remember the conduct of Moses
before Pharaoh. Do not put faith in the benevo-
lence of a priest of idols, nor in the sincerity of a
pretender to wisdom, for these men will hate you
as a destroyer of their livelihood and domination.
Keep a steady watch against being placed in danger
by accepting the caresses of a woman; remember
how Samson was decoyed by Delilah. Do not be
familiar with any woman when alone with her, or
in the dark; remember Orpheus and Eurydice.

Make yourself beloved of women, that they be made happier ; but never love any woman so much that you cannot be happy without her. As to the beings of the elements, the love which they have for a Magus immortalises them, whether Sylphs, Gnomes, Undines, or fiery Salamandrines, but the love of such beings by a Magus is insensate and may destroy him. Be ever intelligent and just to such elemental beings, and you will be rewarded with happiness because of your good actions.

NOTES.

The Eighth Tarot Trump, named Justice, represents a seated female figure robed and crowned, holding a sword in the right hand and a pair of scales in the left hand. Lévi gives as its meaning the equilibrium of attraction and repulsion. P. Christian gives similar meanings, adding in the Physical World it refers to Human Justice, which is always fallible and tinctured with personal motives or personal emotions.

IX

THE HERMIT—L'ERMITE

WHEN the adept has provided himself with the
Magical Sword and Wand, he yet needs a Magical
Lamp whose beams will chase away all the phantoms
of darkness. (The Lamp is figured at p. 103 of the
Rituel of Éliphaz Lévi, but does not quite correspond
to the description here given.) Four metals should
enter into its composition : gold, silver, brass, iron.
The foot of iron, the knot of brass, the reservoir of
silver, and a golden triangle above this, and erect in
the middle ; from each side springs an arm composed
of three tubes of gold, silver, and brass, twisted
together ; there are nine wick burners, three on
each side arm, and three above the triangle over
the reservoir ; upon the iron foot is engraved an
Hermetic triangle, with the symbols of Mercury
above, Sol and Luna below ; around the rim of the
semiglobular base is fixed a brazen serpent ; and above
the globular part, between it and the brazen knot,

there should be an androgyne figure with male and female heads, whose arms are stretched over the globe. Engrave diverse forms on the brass knot; and upon the silver cup must be placed the Hexagram with the letters of the Tetragrammaton in its centre. Upon the golden triangle above engrave a God surrounded by rays, as a symbol of the fecundity of the infinite and eternal. On each side of the reservoir for oil, fix a ring, and hang chains to these rings—one of silver, one of iron; by these chains the lamp may be suspended, or carried by the magician. The wicks for the burners should be of new linen threads, but dyed, the three on the right blue, the three on the left red, and the three middle wicks gold coloured.

The Lamp should be lit from a consecrated fire, but the greatest effect arises when the Lamp burns without wicks and without oil; lighted only by the Lux of the Universal Fluidic Agent, or by one of the material elementals of Water.

The light of this Magical Lamp should work marvels, it should illuminate the consciences of men and women so that you may read them, and should enable you to recognise each type of spiritual being. The magician should not attempt any serious ceremonial until he has grasped the Wand, and illumined the Lamp; just as in common life, if you want to walk safely in the dark, you must carry a candle and try the ground before you with a staff.

NOTES.

The Tarot Trump numbered 9 is named the Hermit. It represents an aged man enveloped in a mantle leaning on a staff, and carrying a lantern. The allotted meanings are wisdom, goodness, and morality, according to Éliphaz Lévi in his *Rituel*.

P. Christian writes: "In the Divine World the meaning is absolute wisdom; in the Intellectual World, prudence; and in the Physical World, circumspection, the proper guide of human actions."

The Magical Lamp is figured by Lévi in his *Rituel* at p. 103.

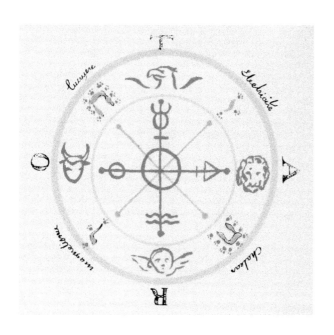

THE WHEEL OF EZEKIEL.

X

THE WHEEL OF FORTUNE—LA ROUE DE FORTUNE

THE Wheel of Ezekiel is the type on which all the Pantacles of the Higher Magic are designed.

When the adept is in the blessed possession of a full knowledge of the powers of the Seal of Solomon, and of the virtues of the Wheel of Ezekiel, which is indeed correspondent, in its entire symbolism, with that of Pythagoras, he has sufficient experience to design talismans and pantacles for any special magical purpose.

The Wheel of Ezekiel contains the solution of the problem of the quadrature of the circle, and demonstrates the correspondences between words and figures, letters and emblems; it exhibits the tetragram of characters analogous to that of the elements and elemental forms. It is a glyph of perpetual motion. The triple ternary is shown; the central point is the first Unity; three circles are added, each with four attributions, and the dodekad is thus seen. The state of universal equilibrium is suggested by the

counterpoised emblems, and the pairs of symbols.
The flying Eagle balances the man ; the roaring Lion
counterpoises the laborious Bull.

Kether, the Crown; Tiphereth, Beauty ; and Yesod,
Foundation, form a central axis ; while Wisdom,
Chokmah, equilibrates with Understanding, Binah ;
and the Severity of Justice, Geburah, makes a counterpoise with the Mercy of Justice, Chesed ; similar
conceptions are the contests between Eros and
Anteros, between Jacob and the Angel, Samael and
Anael, Mars and Venus. The Philosophic Cross
and the Greek monogram of Christos are comparable
also to this magical wheel.

In order that a consecrated talisman shall give
real help to you, it must be well understood, and
the correspondences realised ; for a pantacle is an
ideal materialised, made visible, made portable, and
may contain as much knowledge as a book. It is an
image of some part of God and His works, it is as a
card of the eternal kingdom.

Consider well the aim to be accomplished, and the
powers to be invoked ; select the symbols, emblems,
and letters with the greatest care, seeking Chokmah
and Binah from that spark of the Divine which over-
shadows you, and then trace, mark, or engrave your
chosen design upon a plate of gold, silver, or of

Corinth brass, or cut it on precious stones, or draw it upon virgin parchment. When the work has been skilfully and accurately finished, then submit it to consecration with prayers and invocations of the Four and of the Seven, using suitable perfumes in the incense; after which wrap up the talisman in clean silk and place it in a cedar casket, and it will be effectual to carry it always about with you.

NOTES.

The Tarot Trump marked 10 is named the Wheel of Fortune; the card shows a wheel supported on two upright beams. Hermanubis stands on one side, and Typhon on the other; above is the Sphynx holding a sword in its Lion's jaws. Éliphaz Lévi alleges that Etteilla, who made a superficial study of the Tarot, is answerable for a more modern form of this card, in which the beings around the wheel are a man, a mouse, and a monkey.

The meanings of this Trump are said to be paternity, virile force, manifestation, and principle. P. Christian remarks that on the Physical plane the card points out the varying changes of the so-called fate or fortune.

This key is figured by Lévi in his *Clef des grands mystères*, page 117.

XI

FORTITUDE—STRENGTH—LA FORCE

LISTEN now to the secret of strength. A constant dropping will wear away a stone, and in the end will perforate it. The aim to which you ever devote your will power will be at length attained; you begin to succeed as soon as you begin to will success. Real will power is not a privilege in the hands of the multitude. To exercise true will power you must be free; no one of the multitude is free; to be free is to be the master of your life, and over others. To learn how to will is to learn how to exercise dominion. But to be able to exert will power you must first know; for will power applied to folly is madness, death, and hell.

To mistake the means for the end is an absurdity.

To mistake for the end that which is not even a means is the acme of absurdity.

You are the master of all the events you can

overcome. Things for which you have an imperious need are masters over you.

Things you possess the right to desire, you have the power to obtain.

You must be ever watchful in the exercise of your will, and be heedful that you do not fall into a position of dependence from want of exertion, from simple idleness.

Men who are to contend together in a race must go through a long and severe training.

Magical ceremonies may be regarded as a sort of gymnastic exercise of the will power, and for this reason all the great teachers of the world have recommended them as proper and efficacious. In any religious sect only those who carry out the external observances are reckoned as real supporters of the cause.

The more one does, the more one can do in the future.

To live a life guided by the caprice of the moment is to lead the life of an animal; this may conceivably be a life of innocence, but it is a life of submission.

Those who watch, those who fast, those who pray, those who refrain from pleasure, those who place body at the command of mind, can bring all the powers of nature into subjection to their purposes.

Such as these are the world's masters; such men alone do works which survive them.

Never confound the slaves of superstition and fear with such masters of nature.

To abstain from pleasant things through fear is to enslave the will; such conduct tends to lower rather than to raise your position.

To live like an anchorite, without the superstitious ignorance which leads him to such a course of life, this is wisdom indeed, and power is the reward.

Notes.

The Eleventh Tarot Trump represents an erect female figure, robed and crowned, closing with her naked hands the jaws of a furious lion, and yet showing complete ease and self-possession. Its meaning is persevering strength and indomitable energy. Christian considers that it typifies that Principle which underlies the exhibition of power, and then Moral Force, and lastly Physical Force.

XII

THE HANGED MAN—LE PENDU

THE number Twelve completes a cycle, and this
highly mystical Trump represents the Completion
of the Great Work. This startling design might
be also represented by a cross above a triangle
within a Tau, that is, by four multiplied by three
and enshrined in a Universe.

The pack of Tarot Cards, otherwise the Book of
Taro—which word is an anagram of Rota, a wheel
or cycle—consists in truth of a magical, hieroglyphic
and kabalistic alphabet, to which are added four
decades, and four quaternions, which enshrine the
mystic significance of the Wheel of Ezekiel. The
true aim of the Great Work is to volatilise the fixed
after having accomplished the fixation of the volatile.

By a mystical rectification and a subsequent sub-
limation is the Universal Medicine to be obtained,
and so is also the art of the Transmutation of metals ;
by which art indeed even the most gross and impure

substances may be at once changed into pure and living gold. But no one will succeed in this magical transmutation until he has learned to despise earthly riches, and is content with the holy poverty of the true adept. So, then, if any one attains to this sublime secret, he will treasure it with almost super-human care, and it will so never be divulged to any other human being; it must be self attained. The secret matter of the Philosopher is composed of volatilised Salt, of Mercury which has been fixed, and of purified Sulphur; this perfected Matter is the Azoth of the philosophers. The Salt is only to be volatilised by condensation from the Seven rays of Sol, which are the respective soul essences of the seven metals. The Mercury is fixed by saturation with the Solar essence. The Sulphur is purified by the heat of the Seven luminous rays.

When a man is fully initiated he has a knowledge of all those processes, and he knows that he holds these secrets under the penalty of death. The Taro can preserve you from the danger of such punish-ment, by rendering you incapable of the commission of such a crime. Remember the histories of Prome-theus and of Tantalus. The former stole the sacred fire from heaven and transferred it to the earth. The latter violated the privacy of nature to seize

the secrets of divinity. Remember also the fate of
Ixion, who attempted to ravish the Queen of the Sky.
Remember also the Cross and the Stake. Ponder
over the long martyrdom of Raymond Lully, the
inconceivable sufferings of Paracelsus, the madness
of William Postel, the wandering life and miserable
end of Cornelius Agrippa. Love God, gain wisdom,
and preserve unutterable silence.

NOTES.

The Twelfth Tarot Trump, named the Hanged Man,
is the most closely veiled of all Tarot hieroglyphics.
Its real meaning is now known to but very few ;
there is the gravest doubt whether Lévi knew it
himself. Papus, who has produced a work on the
Tarot, gives a clearly faulty explanation. Neither
Etteilla nor Court de Gebelin grasped the hidden
meaning. But its significance has in some cases
been found by clairvoyant visions, and in a few by
intuition. The key is held by such as know rightly
to which Hebrew letter it belongs and the correspondences of that letter.

The picture shows a man with his hands tied
behind his back, and a rope is seen tied around his
ankles, the other end being attached to a beam, so

that when the card is held with its number at
the top, the man appears to be hung up by his
feet. Lévi in his *Dogme* gives the following state-
ment :—

"This hanged man, then, is the Adept bound by
his engagements, spiritualised, as is shown by his
inverted position. He is Prometheus subjected to
everlasting torture as a punishment for his glorious
theft ; or similarly he is Judas the traitor, and his
sufferings threaten any one who should reveal the
Great Arcanum. Lastly, to the Kabalist, this
hanged man, who corresponds to his twelfth dogma,
that of the Promised Messiah, is a protest against
that Saviour whom the Christians worship, and they
seem to be still saying to Jesus, 'How canst thou
save others, thou who couldst not save thyself ?'"

XIII

DEATH—LA MORT

An effort must now be made to learn the truth
concerning the greatest and most consoling, yet
also the most formidable of the Minor Arcana—
concerning Death. Now, in truth, Death is but a
phantom of your ignorance and fear. Death has
no existence in the Sanctum Regnum of existence.
A change, however awful, demonstrates movement,
and movement is life ; those only who have attempted
to check the disrobing of the spirit have tried to
create a real death. We all are dying and being
renewed every day, because every day our bodies
have changed to some extent. Be troubled lest
you soil and tear your bodily raiment, your coat of
skin, but fear not to leave it aside when the time
has come for a period of repose from the work of
this world.

Leave not your material garment for ever, until
the time for your departure has come ; that is, destroy

not your own life, for it may be that you would
awake to find yourself naked, chill, and ashamed :
it may be too that such a corpse feels its own ne-
cropsy.   Do not attempt to preserve the bodies of
the dead, let nature do her work at once; let there
be no worship of a dead body, for it represents but
the ragged old clothes of a life.

Do not grieve for the beloved dead, for they are
even more alive than you.   If you regret the loss of
their affection and support, you may still love their
memory, and waft messages to them, and perchance
may receive an answer; for by the aid of the Keys
of Solomon the barriers of the thither world, the
plane of disembodied beings, and even of the heaven,
may be raised for a moment.

Understand well that the life-current of the progress of souls is regulated by a law of development,
which carries the individual ever upward, and there
is no tendency to a natural fall.   Souls shall only
fall who elect to descend and choose the evil rather
than the good.   The material plane on which you
live is a prison to you, and if souls fall and come back
to it, they become again imprisoned.

If you desire to communicate with those who have
passed on, you must.

But be warned in time against many deceptions,

for your fancied souls in heaven may be but phantoms of the air; elementaries, shadows of humanity energised by elemental beings; mere senseless astral forms, and of no more value than the mirage of dreams.

Necromancy, and Goetia, which is Evil Magic, do produce such shells and demons, apparitions of deceit. If, however, you are an adept of the True White Higher school, you will at all times condemn and challenge the practice of such fatal science.

The only possible mode of communion with souls of a higher sphere, who have passed beyond the terrestrial aura by reason of the change called Death, is by dream or ecstasy; but on waking to common consciousness there will be no recollection present in the mind of what has passed, because, owing to the change of plane, each idea necessarily suffers a change of form—a recurrence of the dream, or a return to the ecstasy, recalls what has gone before.

It is a curious fact that most persons fail to remember anything of good and happy dreams, even although they do often recall dreams of sin and folly and absurdity; the reason being that these latter are more closely, and good ideals are less closely, related to our very materially minded lives on earth.

Now if the purely minded adept and pupil of the Higher Magic does seriously aspire to communion with a soul on the plane above him, the true way is as follows.

But again you must take warning that unless the aspirant is pure, and strong with health, and wise in procedure, there will be grave risk of disordering the mind, or of catalepsy, or even of death.

Every puerile and commonplace thought must be banished from the mind, for if this be not done, and if a ceremony of such awful solemnity be entered upon lightly, frivolously, or from a vain curiosity, there will come a moment when the dread " King of Earth " will appear and punish. The mind and emotions must then be raised to a pitch of sublime exaltation proceeding from a pure and disinterested love. Bring to remembrance all the sweet sayings of the departed one, formulate her aims and good efforts, collect around you all that belonged to her and reminds you of her face, form, and personality. Observe the dates of her birth and death (and of any special events which have drawn you two together); choose such a day. Prepare for this date by daily retiring to a quiet room, if possible where she has lived, or where she has been, and pass an hour there in darkness, or at least with the eyes shut, pondering over her words and ideas, conversing in imagination with her as listening to her conceived answers. When the day comes near you must for seven days, and should for even fourteen days, abstain rigorously from useless communications with other persons, from follies, from demonstrations of affection to all others, and from every form of physical and mental excess; take but one meal a day, and drink no stimulant nor narcotic liquids.

When the fateful day has come, take a portrait of the beloved one, a sun picture is the best (photograph), or if a painting, it should be one executed with the greatest care and detail. With great care and delicacy ˙ prepare the room and the collected objects which have belonged to the deceased, make them all spotlessly clean, and give especial care to the portrait; place it in a good position, and decorate the frame with the flowers she loved. During the day you should pass several hours in the chamber alone, seated in contemplation of the portrait and the ideas and reminiscences of the dead friend.

When the even has come you must bathe, and clothe yourself in clean linen, and put on a white mantle. Enter the sacred chamber, fasten the door and perform the Conjuration of the Four Elements. Upon a chafing-dish you then burn wood of the laurel, with aloes and incense. There must be no other light in the room. When the wood and incense have burned down and the fire is at the point of extinction, then in a deep and solemn voice call three times in succession upon the name of the beloved dead one. This you must do with all your force of heart and of spirit, with intense will power; close the eyes, cover them with the hands, sink on your knees and pray.

Then at last, after a solemn pause, call softly and with sweet voice the name of the loved one three times; and open your eyes, and see———.

NOTES.

The Tarot Trump, No. xiii., is named Death, and represents a human skeleton, armed with a scythe, mowing the grassy soil, upon which are seen human remains. To this Lévi in his *Rituel* assigns the meanings dominion and power, rebirth, creation, and destruction.

P. Christian writes: " In the Divine World the meaning is constant change of form; in the Intellectual World, the ascent of human spirit to divine spheres; and in the Physical World, natural death following decay of the material envelope."

XIV

TEMPERANCE—LA TEMPERANCE

If you desire long life and health avoid all excesses, carry nothing to extremes. Once more preserve the equilibrium; you must neither abandon yourself to the benignities of Chesed, nor restrict yourself to the rigours of Geburah.

So when you have passed beyond the mortal sphere by the allurements of ecstasy, return to yourself, seek repose and enjoy the pleasures which life supplies for the wise, but do not indulge too freely.

If you feel fatigued by the tempting fascination of a prolonged fast, then take food and drink; but if you have loss of appetite from generous diet, then fast by all means. If you are feeling the seductiveness of womankind, seek relief from women.

You must learn to overcome all passions, and conquer all tendencies to folly. But let there be no misunderstanding. To vanquish an enemy there must be no running away: true victory can only follow meeting him face to face, joining in a struggle, and so showing your command over him.

It is related of Paracelsus that he became intoxicated daily, and sobered himself by violent exercise; thus he was found strong as a man with *sangfroid*, and yet possessing all the animation of alcoholic stimulation.

You should repose for as long a period as is expended in the preparations for and in the actual operations of magic; spend the hours of rest upon the bosom of Mother Nature, and in the chaste embrace of Nature's sweet restorer, Sleep.

Pass alternately from the triangle to the circle, and from the circle to the triangle.

Temperate the wine with water, and rectify the water with wine. Wine is the emblem of Truth; yet it is not well to pour out either, in pure form, to ordinary men and women; some dilution with water is very desirable. Know that the Luminous Septenary has as its enemies, and as obstacles, but acting also in some ways as auxiliaries, a Dark Septenary of averse forces.

If a man abuses the high forces of the Septenary of Powers, his errors form the Seven Capital Sins.

Give but little wine to one who easily gets intoxicated; and, in like manner, give but little occult instruction to those who make light of it, who abuse instead of use, and so change truth into error.

Notes.

The Fourteenth Tarot Trump, named Temperance, shows the Angel of Occult Wisdom and Power holding a goblet in each hand, and pouring from one into the other the two essences whose union form the Elixir of Life.

Lévi in his *Rituel* assigns to this card the meanings of the heaven of the Sun, temperatures, seasons, motions, and the chances and changes of life.

P. Christian remarks that the figure represents the genius of the Sun ; in the Divine World, the perpetual alternations of life ; in the Intellectual World, the creation of ideas which constitute the moral life ; and in the Physical World, the combinations of natural forces.

XV

SATAN—THE DEVIL—LE DIABLE

COME hither now and let us consider without fear this great one, the bugbear of the Christian creed, this ghost of Ahriman, the monstrous androgynous sphynx of Mendes; it is the synthesis of unbalanced forces—a Demon.

The Devil is truly Blind Force. If you help the blind, you may be served by him; if you let the blind lead, you are lost.

Each element and every number has its demon, because each element and every number enshrines a force which ignorance may put to evil purposes. The same sword by which you defend your father, may also slay him.

Know then that the demonic force of each entity must be conquered by knowledge and good purpose. Avoid darkness where demonic power prefers to manifest; fight it in broad daylight, and fearlessly. The Devil, one day, desiring to stop the progress of

an adept, broke one wheel of his chariot; but this
true adept compelled the Devil to curl himself up
on the wheel and act for the time as its tire, and so
drove on, reaching his destination even sooner than
he would have done if the Devil had let him alone.

Meditate deeply on this old allegorical epigram,
Aude et Tace, and when you have seized its occult
sense, tell no other of your success.

The symbolic representation of the Devil shows
a multiple, disharmonious and anarchic sort of
sphynx, typical of confusion and disorder. Note
this maxim :—A devil is a magnetic current consisting of a concourse of blind and perverse wills.

When certain superstitious mystics relegated intelligence and reason to the Devil, they reversed the
Absolute. That is to say, they chose as their God
him who was truly the Devil, and they attributed
the malice of Satan to the True God.

There is no child with even ordinary sense who
is not more learned than the Devil.

The Devil is even of lower grade than the beings
of the Elements. He is doubtless more powerful, but
he is as blind as poor Samson became. But to enable
the Devil to pull down the pillars of a temple, you
would have to lead him to the pillars and say to him,
There they are.

No true Magician ever made any attempt to evoke the Devil, for he knows where the Devil is always to be found ; but he may order the Devil to work—and the Devil obeys.

In Black Magic, the Devil means the employment of the Grand Magical Agent for a wicked purpose by a perverted Will.

NOTES.

The Fifteenth Tarot Trump is said by Lévi to be the only one that Etteilla understood. This Etteilla was an *illuminé* hairdresser who published a work on the Tarot, making grave alterations of the designs collected by Court de Gebelin, a much more reliable authority. His true name was Alliette.

The card shows an altar upon which stands a demon in human form, to which are added horns, long goat ears, and bat-like wings; he holds a torch in his left hand ; two smaller demons, one male the other female, stand on the ground beside the altar. Some authors say the figure is that of Baphomet, the idol which the Knight Templars were said to worship.

Christian alleges that this demon represents the Typhon of Egypt, the genius of misfortune ; and as related to the three worlds it refers to Predestination, Mystery, and Fatality.

XVI

THE TOWER—LA MAISON DE DIEU

Do you know why the Fiery Sword of Samael is stretched over the Garden of Delight, which was the cradle of our race?

Do you know why the Deluge was ordered to efface from the earth every vestige of the race of the giants?

Do you know why the Temple of Solomon was destroyed?

These events have been necessary because the Great Arcanum of the Knowledge of Good and of Evil has been revealed.

Angels have fallen because they have attempted to divulge this Great Secret. It is the secret of Life, and when its first word is betrayed, that word becomes fatal. If the Devil himself were to utter that Word, he would die.

This Word will destroy each one who speaks it, and every one who hears it spoken. If it were spoken aloud in the hearing of the people of a town, that town would be given over to Anathema. If that Word were to be whispered beneath the dome of a Temple, then within three days the Temple doors would fly open, a Voice would utter a cry, the divine indweller would depart, and the building would fall in ruins. No refuge could be found for one who revealed it; if he mounted to the topmost part of a tower the lightning-flash would strike him, if he tried to hide himself in the caverns of the earth, a torrent would whirl him away; if he sought refuge in the house of a friend he would be betrayed; if in the arms of the wife of his bosom, she would desert him in affright.

In his passion of despair he would renounce his science and knowledge, and, condemning himself to the same blindness as did Œdipus, would shriek out —"I have profaned the bed of my mother."

Happy is the man who solves the Enigma of the Sphynx, but wretched is he who retails the answer to another.

He who has solved the secret and guards its secrecy is as the "King of Earth"; he disdains mere riches, is inaccessible to any suffering or fear from destiny, he could await with a smile the crash of worlds. This secret is, moreover, profaned and falsified by its mere revelation, and never yet has a just or true idea come from its betrayal. Those who possess it have found it. Those who pronounce it for others to hear have lost it—already.

NOTES.

The Tarot Trump numbered 16, and called Le Maison de Dieu upon cards made on the Continent, is commonly known in this country as the Tower of Babel. It represents a tower struck by lightning; two men are seen falling headlong; these are said to be intended for Nimrod and his chief minister.

Lévi assigns several meanings to this card; weakness, changes, subversions, and the heaven of Luna.

Christian explains this card as meaning the punishment of pride, the ruin of such as impiously attempt to penetrate the secrets of divinity, and on the human plane, the occasional reverses of fortune.

XVII

THE STAR—ÐETOILE

You must become thoroughly acquainted with the planets and also with the fixed stars. When their names are mastered, their influences must be learned; you must discover the particular hours and in what sign the Psyche of the World pours forth from her two goblets the waters of life like two rivers.

Learn both day and night hours, in order that you may select such as are most suitable for the work you wish to perform.

The midnight hour is marked by the special tendency toward the appearance of phantoms. The first and second hours, which follow, are solemn and sad for those who are ill or are sleepless. During the third hour the sufferer from insomnia falls asleep; the fourth, fifth, and sixth are calm, and lead to a healthy repose in sleep.

The seventh and eighth hours of morning are of a voluptuous nature; the ninth, tenth, and eleventh are very suitable for works of friendship; the mid-day hour is a time of heedlessness and languor in summer, and of a sense of well-being in winter.

You should find your own particular Planet in the sky; your intuition should guide you in discovering it; and when found you should salute it with reverence every night that you see it shining down upon you. The genius of this star must be invoked in your conjurations, and the allotted name of the star may be worked out by means of the learned tables and Kabalistic permutations designed by Trithemius and Agrippa.

You should then make a talisman of sympathy to connect the planetary forces with yourself; make it of the metal of the planet which presided at your birth (the lord of the ascendant of your natus); engrave upon this plate of metal the sign of the Microcosm with the numbers of your name, the numbers related to the planet or star, and the name of the genius.

When you are seeking divine inspiration gaze at your star, holding the talisman with your left hand pressing it against your heart; if it be daytime, or the star be invisible, gaze upon the talisman itself, and recite the name of the genius or spirit of the star, three times.

E

When you see the star become brilliant and glitter in response to your aspiration, be of good hope for success ; but should it be seen to pale at your glance, then be very prudent and take the greatest care of yourself.

The Tarot Trump numbered 17 is called the Star. It represents an entirely nude female figure kneeling on land and sea, and pouring a liquid out of a vase in each hand ; the streams form a river at her feet. Above is a star of eight rays, and seven smaller stars surround it. There is a bushy tree growing at her right side, and upon it the bird of Hermes has alighted.

The meanings given to this Tarot Trump by Lévi are : Immortality, thought, the influence of idea upon form, the heaven of the soul.

Christian gives as its meanings : Immortality, the internal illumination which guides men to choose the better path, and hope. He says the figure is represented nude to point out that even when man is robbed of all his possessions, he may still retain hope.

XVIII

THE MOON—LA LUNE

THE Moon exercises a very considerable amount of influence upon the magnetic fluid of the earth, as is shown by the ebb and flow of the waters of the seas; you should then examine carefully the effects of the influences of the Moon in her several phases, and take note of the days and hours of the Moon's course. The quarter of the New Moon is favourable for the commencement of all magical enterprises; the first quarter gives an influence of heat, the full moon an influence of dryness, and the last quarter a cold influence.

These are the special characters of the days of the Moon, distinguished by the twenty-two Tarot Keys and the signs of the Seven Planets.

> I. The Juggler, or the Magus. The first day of
> the Lunar course: the Moon was created,
> says Rabbi Moses, on the fourth day.

II. The Gnosis, or La Papesse. The second day, whose genius is named Enodiel, the fish and birds were created; it is propitious for the works of occult science.

III. The Mother, or Empress. The third day saw the creation of humanity. The Kabalists often call the Moon by the name Mother, and allot the number three to her: this day is propitious for generation.

IV. The Despot, or Emperor. The fourth day is baneful, for on this day Cain was born; but it is a powerful day for unjust and tyrannical acts.

V. The Pope, or Priest. The fifth is a day of happiness; it was the birthday of Abel.

VI. The Lovers, or the Struggle. Birth of Lamech, a day marked by contest and anger; suitable for conspirators and for revolt.

VII. The Chariot. Birth of Hebron; a day very propitious for religious ceremonial.

VIII. Justice. Death of Abel; the day of expiation.

IX. The Hermit. Birth of Methuselah; a day of joy for children.

X. The Wheel of Fortune. Birth of Nebuchadnezzar; a day for conjurations of plagues; a baneful day: reign of brute force.

XI. Strength. Birth of Noah. The visions of the day are deceitful; but children born this day are healthy and long lived.

XII. The Hanged Man, the Tau. Birth of Samael; a day favourable for Kabalah and prophecy, and for the accomplishment of the Great Work.

XIII. Death. Birth of Canaan, the cursed son of Ham; an evil day and an evil number.

XIV. Temperance. Benediction of Noah. On this day Cassiel of the hierarchy of Auriel presides.

XV. The Devil, or Typhon. Birth of Ishmael; a day of reproof and exile.

XVI. The Tower. Birth of Esau and Jacob; the latter is predestined to ruin Esau.

XVII. The Star. The Ruin of Sodom and Gomorrah; this day is under the rule of Scorpio. Health for the good, ruin for evil persons; dangerous when it falls on a Saturday.

XVIII. The Moon. Birth of Isaac; a day of good augury.

XIX. The Sun. Birth of Pharaoh ; a day of danger.

XX. The Judgment. Birth of Judah ; a day propitious for divine revelations.

XXI. The World or the Sphynx. Birth of Saul ; a day for physical force and material prosperity.

XXII. Saturn. The birth of Job.

XXIII. Venus. The birth of Benjamin.

XXIV. Jupiter. The birth of Japhet.

XXV. Mercury. The Tenth plague of Egypt.

XXVI. Mars. The passage of the Red Sea by the Israelites.

XXVII. Luna. The victory of Judas Maccabeus.

XXVIII. Sol. Samson carries off the gates of Gaza.

XXIX. The Tarot Trump called Le Fou, the unwise man ; a day of abortion.

NOTES.

The Tarot Trump, No. xviii., represents the Moon in the sky letting fall drops of dew ; below is the land on which stand two towers, and between them are a dog and a wolf ; in the foreground is water in which a crayfish is swimming.

The occult meanings ascribed to this trump by Lévi are : The elements, the visible world, reflected light and symbolism.

Christian says that the meanings are the abyss of the infinite ; the shadow which enshrouds the human ego when it accepts the rule of the instincts unchecked by spiritual aims ; and on the lowest plane, the assaults of hidden enemies.

XIX

THE SUN—LE SOLEIL

THE Sun is the centre and source of all high Magical force, and this force nourishes and renews without pause that latent Light which is the grand agent manifested in magnetism and vital energy.

The Sun is the central and yet universal magnet of the stars. It has two poles, one possessing attractive force and the other repulsive force; it is alone by the balance of these two energies that it maintains cosmic equilibrium and universal motion. The Sun it is which bestows radiance upon the planets and meteors, it is of the principle of Fire, and in this world it is the source of the phosphorescence of the sea and even of the scintillation of the glow-worm. It is the heat of the Sun which constitutes the stimulant essence of the generous wine from the fruit of the grape, and which brings to perfection the luscious sweetness of all fruits. It is the Sun which awakens the dormant energies of all beings in spring time, and which prompts to the enjoyment of all the sweet mysteries of sexual love. It is the Sun's force which courses in our veins and palpitates in our hearts, and it is the light of the Sun which empurples our blood and makes it resemble the purple redness of wine. The Sun is the sanctuary of spiritual beings who have been loosed from the ties of earth life, and there is the blazing tabernacle in which resides the Soul of the Messiah. You place your altars where the Sun's rays fall upon them, and renew the sacred fire upon them from its rays. When you consecrate a talisman or pantacle you open up a path along which a solar ray may pass thence into it during the ceremonial.

When the adept seeks to heal the sick or relieve any pain he raises his hands towards the Light and Heat of the Sun, and then lowering them he touches the sick man, saying, "Be thou healed if thou hast faith and will." The perfumed flowers and leaves to be used as incense should be dried in the Sun's rays, notwithstanding the fact that flowers and leaves gathered in darkness have more potency than those plucked by daylight; because plants exhale their aroma in sunlight, and close up their pores to preserve it during the absence of the creating rays. Gold is the special metal of Sol, and it tends to augment the solar force in all with which it is brought into contact.

A golden lamen applied to the forehead renders the mind more open to and receptive of divine influences.

A golden talisman worn on the breast over the heart increases the force of emotions which are good and benevolent, while it tends to banish impure passions.

Notes.

The Nineteenth Trump represents the Sun shining above in the heavens and casting its rays upon two children, who stand holding each other's hands; a wall of masonry is seen behind them. In some old cards this wall is garlanded with flowers.

The meanings given elsewhere by Lévi are: The Prince of the heavens, the summit, the head: he remarks that some examples of this card show a child mounted on a white horse and waving a scarlet banner. Christian believes that this Trump represents the passage from earth life to that of the unknown future.

XX

THE LAST JUDGMENT—LE JUGEMENT

THESE are the Privileges and the Powers of a Magus ; and first are recited the Seven Grand Privileges :—

Aleph. 1. He sees God and is able to commune with the Seven Genii around the throne.

Beth. 2. He is above the influence of all pains and fears.

Ghimel. 3. He has authority over High Spiritual Powers, and can command Infernal forces.

Daleth. 4. He is the master over his own life, and can influence the lives of other men.

Heh. 5. He can never be taken unawares, nor weakened, nor overcome.

Vau. 6. He understands the reasons for the Present, the Past, and the Future.

Zain. 7. He holds the secret of what is meant by the Resurrection from the dead.

The Seven Major Powers are :—

Cheth. 1. The power of making the Philosopher's Stone.

Teth. 2. The possession of the Universal Medicine.

Yod. 3. The knowledge of the mode of Perpetual Motion, and of the Quadrature of the Circle.

Kaph. 4. The power of changing any base matter into gold.

Lamed. 5. The ability to coerce wild beasts, and to charm serpents.

Mem. 6. To possess the Notorial Art and to have universal knowledge.

Nun. 7. The power of discoursing with knowledge and learning upon any subject, even without previous study.

The Seven Minor Powers are :—

Samech. 1. To know in a moment the hidden thoughts of any man or woman.

Ayin. 2. To compel any one to act with sincerity.

Peh. 3. To foresee any future events which do not depend upon the will of a superior being.

Tzaddi. 4. To give instantly wise counsel and acceptable consolation.

Qoph. 5. To be always calm and content in the most grievous adversity.

Resh. 6. Never to feel love or hatred unless it is designed.

Shin. 7. To possess the secret of constant wealth, and never to fall into destitution or misery.

These Privileges are the final degree of Human Perfectibility ; these are open to attainment by the elect, by those who can dare, by those who would never abuse them, and who know when to be silent.

Tau. In conclusion, Magi can control the elemental forces, calm tempests, heal the sick, and raise the dead. But these things are sealed with the triple Seal of Solomon : initiates know of them, this is sufficient ; as to other persons, whether they deride you, or whether they are overcome with fear at your audacity, what matters it to you ?

Notes.

Lévi gives the whole of this chapter in his *Dogme*, pages 79–83, as a quotation —perhaps from this treatise.

This Twentieth Tarot Trump shows, at first sight, a representation of the judgment day. An angel blowing a trumpet and carrying a banner is flying overhead. Below is seen a figure with his back toward the observer, rising from a tomb. On each side is an imposing human figure, one male and one female, who also seem to be rising from the earth. Lévi gives as its meaning the generative force of the earth, vegetable life, and eternal life.

Christian describes this card as a symbol of the resurrection.

XXI

THE UNWISE MAN—LE MAT

Do not ally yourself either in affection or interest
with any one who is not an earnest student of the
higher life, unless you can completely dominate him,
and even then be sure that you either recompense or
chastise him according to his deserts ; for the profane
person hears many truths, but understands none; his
ears are large but have no discretion. The profane
passes his life in giddy risks, deluded with vain desires, listening to imaginary promptings, and with
his eyes fixed on fancied sights. You may think he
is pleased with your aims, but the truth is that he
is absorbed by his own follies; the profane has no
appreciation of the truth, and feels no real affection.
The profane is imprudent and shameless ; he discloses
things which should be kept concealed, and attracts
to himself brute forces which may devour him. That
which he most neglects is himself; he wears his
vices as a blazon, but they are all over present burden

to him, yet he does not recognise that they are a constant source of weakness. Make it a definite rule of life always to avoid :—

1. Such as are ever judging and condemning their parents, who despise their fathers and have no true affection for their mothers.

2. All men who show no courage, and all women who have not modesty.

3. Those who do not maintain their friendships.

4. Those who ask for advice, and then do not take it.

5. Those who are never in the wrong.

6. Those who are always seeking the impossible, and who are obstinately unjust to others.

7. Those who, when danger is present, seek only their own safety.

All such persons are neither worthy of your confidence nor of your love. Fear contamination from them ; avoid them. Yet even as you yourself must also avoid the follies of life, be careful not to put yourself in an attitude of superiority to the conditions of existence merely from a false pride, and never stoop to debase yourself to the level of the brute creation ; rise above the common ways of life, and never become the slave of custom and conventionality. Treat the habits of ordinary life as others treat the weaknesses of childhood.   Amuse the crowd to prevent personal injury, but never address it except in parables and enigmas; such has been the mode of conduct of all the great Masters of Magic, and in such an attitude there is wisdom.

NOTES.

We are now met by an unexpected difficulty, for Lévi has written this chapter No. 21, following No. 20, the Judgment, without any notification that the card referred to is not that numbered 21, which is the Universe, but the sole unnumbered Trump of the set.   Of other authors, some have numbered the Universe Moon or Fool as 0 or as the 22nd.   The fact remains that in all packs the Universe is numbered 21, and it will in this tract be considered after the next chapter, which clearly refers to it.

In this chapter, where an author refers so much to the profane, the Trump Le Fou is clearly indicated.   It represents a wayfarer walking along a road and carrying a burden slung over his shoulder; he has a staff in his right hand.   Behind, he is attacked by a tiger which has already fastened on his clothing, while his face shows that he is as yet ignorant of its attack.   In his *Rituel*, Lévi assigns to this trump the somewhat incongruous meanings of the sensitive, the flesh, and eternal life.

Christian gives another description of this card. Instead of the design described above, he says that the 20th trump should represent a blind man carrying a wallet and coming into contact with a broken obelisk, upon which is couched a crocodile with gaping jaws; the meaning assigned by him is the inevitable punishment of sin. This blind man, he says, is the symbol of humanity, which is the blind slave of matter. He numbers this card o, but places it between numbers 20 and 21.

F

XXII

THE UNIVERSE—LE MONDE

Do you now understand the Enigma of the Sphynx?

Do you know the thought which exists in its human head? the love which pervades its woman's bosom? the labour denoted by the loins of the bull? the struggle which the lion's claws can wage? the beliefs and the poesy of its eagle's wings? Yes, you know that the Sphynx refers to Man.

But do you know that the Sphynx is one and alone, and remains unchanged, while as to man,—is not each one a Sphynx of a different synthesis? In some there is the head of a Lion, such as is drawn on talismans of Fire; these are descendants of the Salamanders. Others have the head of a Bull, or of an Eagle or Ibis. Each of these has its divine counterpart, and this it is which the wise men of Egypt depicted in those hieroglyphic figures which the profane scholars of our time find so ridiculous and misleading.

May they be forgiven from the recesses of the Tomb of the divine Hermes.

It is by reason of this diversity of divine inspiration, and its influence over the human will, that the wise have formed such diversified pantacles and talismans. All initiates have had faith in the efficacy of symbols and emblems. How else could the Word be expressed without letters and characters, and why should not letters and characters express the power of the Word they represent.

Write the words "I love" upon a golden jewel and wear it upon the breast; then every time you feel its touch, will not the idea of your love arise in the mind? and I tell you that this jewel, magnetised by your will and your faith, will deflect from you and will extinguish all the attacks directed against you. If you pass through the heat of fire, this will be as a breeze of fresh air to you. If you are in danger of drowning, this will bear you up amid the waters. Never then condemn the use of amulets, pantacles, talismans, and phylacteries. Unfortunate is the man who is not impressed by the appearance of any image, and who does not bow his head before any symbol.

But each wise man should have his phylactery or talisman, as every Master has his clavicule. Such are the talismans of Hermes; there are others of

Solomon, of Rabbi Chaël, and of Thetel; there are other signs used by Paracelsus, by Agrippa, and Albertus Magnus.

The symbols of Abraham the Jew gave rise to the emblematic designs of Nicholas Flamel, which again differ from those of Basil Valentine and Bernard of Treves.

All embody the same ideas, but according to the special form of consecration speak another idiom of the language of the hieroglyphics.

If you become initiated you will at length make and vary your own talismans and pantacles; you will choose the proper hours, select your perfumes and compose your own invocations, upon the models you may find among the various clavicules of Solomon. Ponder carefully over this axiom: "The man who addresses to a Power unknown to him words which he does not fully comprehend, makes a tenebrous prayer to the spirit of darkness; in other words, he invokes the devil. All that happens in the world, that is devoid of justice and right, has the devil for its author. Remember also that he who consults the oracles abdicates in some part his liberty and makes an appeal to fateful forces.

The true sage directs or corrects the oracle but he never consults it. Saul was already conquered and lost when he consulted the Witch of Endor. In the difficulties of life consult in preference the Sphynx.

Is it a decision that is needed, ask it from the human head.

Is it affection that you desire, ask it of the woman's breast.

Is it help and protection that you need, ask the Lion's claws to afford it.

Are you poor and ignorant, invoke the power of the Bull, and work yourself.

Do the struggles of life weary you, take the Eagle's wings and raise yourself on high above the earth.

The Sphynx only devours those who fail to comprehend her; she will obey any one who has learned the answer to her riddle.

All the forces of Nature correspond to human forces, and are dependent on the will in its sphere of action : constant use of will power extends the sphere of its action.

Man (and by man I do not intend either fools or profane persons)—man is worth whatever he believes himself to be worth ; he can do whatever he believes himself capable of doing ; he does whatever he really desires to do ; he may at length become all that he wills to be.

He, who was not mad, and yet could say, "I am the only Son of God," was the only Son of God. Examples of the past may be re-acted at any time: the types are still existent, and can be brought again into action.

Would you become a Moses, or an Elias?

Would you re-live the career of Paracelsus or of Raymond Lulli? Then learn all that they knew, put your faith in the doctrines they believed, do the acts they did; while awaiting the result, be sober in body, calm in mind, work and pray.

THE KABALISTIC PRAYER

BE favourable to me, oh ye Powers of the Kingdom Divine.

May Glory and Eternity be in my left and right hands, so that I may attain to Victory.

May Pity and Justice restore my soul to its original purity.

May Understanding and Wisdom Divine conduct me to the imperishable Crown.

Spirit of Malkuth, Thou who hast laboured and hast overcome ; set me in the Path of Good.

Lead me to the two pillars of the Temple, to Jakin and Boaz, that I may rest upon them.

Angels of Netzach and of Hod, make ye my feet to stand firmly on Yesod.

Angel of Gedulah, console me.   Angel of Geburah, strike, if it must be so, but make me stronger, so that I may become worthy of the influence of Tiphereth.

Oh Angel of Binah, give me Light.

Oh Angel of Chokmah, give me Love.

Oh Angel of Kether, confer upon me Faith and Hope.

Spirits of the Yetziratic World, withdraw me from the darkness of Assiah.

Oh luminous triangle of the World of Briah, cause me to see and understand the mysteries of Yetzirah and of Atziluth.

Oh Holy Letter **ש**, Shin.

Oh ye Ishim, assist me by the name Shadai.

Oh ye Kerubim, give me strength through Adonai.

Oh Beni Elohim, be brothers unto me in the name of Tzabaoth.

Oh Elohim, fight for me by the Holy Tetragrammaton.

Oh Melakim, protect me through Jehovah.

Oh Seraphim, give me holy love in the name Eloah.

Oh Chashmalim, enlighten me by the torches of Eloi and the Shekinah.

Oh Aralim, angels of power, sustain me by Adonai.

Oh Ophanim, Ophanim, Ophanim, forget me not, and cast me not out of the Sanctuary.

Oh Chaioth ha Kadosh, cry aloud as an eagle, speak as a man, roar and bellow.

Kadosh, Kadosh, Kadosh, Shadai.

Adonai, Jehovah, Ehyeh asher Ehyeh.

Hallelu-Jah.   Hallelu-Jah.

Hallelu-Jah.

       Amen.   Amen.   Amen.

This prayer should be made use of every morning and evening, and it should be recited as a preliminary to all grand magical and Kabalistic ceremonials; it should be recited when facing the orient with the eyes raised to the heavens, or fixed on the Kabalistic emblem of the sublime Tetragrammaton, which you will find drawn for your instruction on an accompanying page.

So soon as you apply both body and soul to the Higher Magic you will have to defend yourself against all the blind forces of the world and of Hades. Earth will send the Bacchantes of Orpheus and the temptresses who assailed Samson and Solomon, even the stones will rise up and hurl themselves at you; Hades will send its Larvæ and Phantoms to attack you. As a defence you will possess the Divine Word, the aura, the magical sword, the magnetic wand, the consecrated water, and the sacred fire, but above all the vigilant power of your invocation.

If you are Royal you may rely upon revolts and counterplots to force the spiritual powers to obey you. Perform the conjuration of the Four by means of the Pantacle of Ezekiel, and proceed by the Septenary and the Triadic method, and by the Pantacle of the Hexagram of Solomon, which latter is the Symbol of the Macrocosm.

For the conjuration of the Tetrad, the Four, you bring into action the powers of the four elements duly consecrated, and you must trace in the air and upon the earth the pentagrams of fire and of water; then make four expirations of the breath, and recite— making the cross—Nicksa, Ghob, Paralda, Djin.

Fluat udor per Spiritum Elohim.

Let the waters flow on, through the spiritual energy from Elohim, or ye Undines must roll back through the influence of this consecrated water.

Maneat terra per Adam.

Let the earth remain solid through Adam. Work, ye Gnomes, as I will, or return to the earth in which I can imprison you by this Pantacle.

Fiat firmamentum per Elohim.

The firmament must persist through the Elohim. Submit, ye Sylphs, or pass away by the current of my breathing.

Fiat judicium per ignem.

Let the decree be carried out by the Fire. Ye Salamanders, be calm, or be coerced by the sacred fire.

You may formulate the Undine as an angelic form with the eyes of death; the Gnome as a winged bull, the Sylph as an eagle chained, and the Salamander as a gliding serpent.

Latin Invocation.

O caput mortuum impero tibi per vivium Serpentem
Kerub impero tibi per Adam
Aquila impero tibi per alas Tauri.
Serpens impero tibi per Angelum et Leonem.

The Conjuration of the Heptad—the Seven, is made with the Magical Wand and fumigations by means of the Seven Planetary Spirits.

Planetary Conjuration.

In the name of Michael, whom Jehovah decrees to command Satan!

In the name of Gabriel, whom Adonai decrees to command Beelzebub!

In the name of Raphael obey Elohim, thou Sachabiel.

By Samael Tzabaoth, and by the name of Elohim Gibur, lay down thy weapons, thou Adramelek.

By Zachariel and Sachiel Melek, submit to the power of Eloah, thou Samgabiel.

In the divine and human name of Shadai, and by
the power of Anael, of Adam and of Chavah, thou
Lilith retire, leave us in peace, thou Nahemah.

By the holy Elohim, and by the power of Orifiel,
in the names of the spirits Cassiel, Schaltiel, Aphiel,
and Zarahiel, turn back, thou Moloch, there are no
children here for thee to devour.

——

You must then trace in the air and upon the earth,
with the Magical Wand, the famous and powerful
Hexagram, the Seal of Solomon.

——

The Conjuration of the Three is performed with
the Tetragrammaton, pronouncing three times in a
deep sonorous voice the Three letters of the Great
Name, tracing in the air and upon the earth the
signs of the four radii of the Wheel of Ezekiel's
Vision, with the words Yod, Heh, Vau, Heh, and
then make the sign of the Cross.

——

You should well understand that the names Satan,
Beelzebub, and others like them, do not mean spiritual
personalities, but rather legions of impure spirits.

My name is Legion, said the Spirit of darkness,
because we are numberless ; in hell, the kingdom of
anarchy, it is number which makes law, and progress

is inverse; for there the most degraded are the least
intelligent and most weak. Thus the law of fatality
compels the demons to descend when they believe
and wish to rise; and so those whom I call the
Chiefs are the most powerless and the most con-
temptible of them all.

Those evil spirits which form the crowd, tremble
before a Chief who is unknown, implacable, and deaf,
never speaking, and whose arm is always raised to
strike. To this phantom are given the names of
Lucifer, Adramelek, and Belial; but this phantom
is but the shadow of God disfigured by their per-
versity, and remains among them to torment and
terrify them for ever.

Be guarded in the words you speak. Speak not of
God, unless you are illuminated. All the images
which you create, whether of God or of other ideals,
remain imprinted on that luminous medium—the
Astral Light of the soul, and of the world; and
there is that Book of the Conscience which shall be
opened and its records revealed in the Last Day.

Know that the Human Brain, although it receives,
does not make any visible record of impressions;
otherwise they would be engraved upon the grey
matter of the Brain and anatomists would see them
there.

The nerve substance does but perceive and collect, by reason of this essence (the Astral Light), the living and ineffaceable pictures of the spiritual atmosphere which you evoke. You may even by sympathy, present or past, with the desires, evoke the impressions of other persons; and thus it is that you can communicate with those who are dead and even perceive the bodily form they have thrown aside, and which they must retake when the grand Consummation arrives and the world is transfigured.

To such as ask you where Paradise and Hell are situated, you should answer: Paradise exists wherever you speak the truth, and do the right; Hell is present wherever you speak that which is false, or do that which is evil.

Paradise and Hell are not localities, they are states, and the contrasted states will remain to eternity; even as good must ever remain in opposition to evil; as the essential of a personality is opposed to that of Intelligent Existence, which is Liberty.

The plastic universal medium, the unsubstantial substance, which is light, motion, and life, this androgyne magnetic force, receives, preserves, and communicates all the forms and images which are the impressions of the Word: this it is which gives form and colour to plants; it is this which stamps upon the fruit of a mother's womb the impress of her thoughts and desires.

It is this which produces apparitions and the sensible visions of exaltation and ecstasy when Superior Spiritual Powers communicate to us by the correspondences of the Word, or when Inferior spirits seek to mount to our plane by sympathy with our grosser passions.

There is no real isolation in this world, there is no point of form and no variety of thought which has not its correspondence, item by item, through analogy, with that which is above, as well as that which is below, in the infinite and finite worlds. This is the true ideal of the mystical Ladder of Jacob whose rungs are bound together by the two Pillars of Light, and which provide for the unbroken circulation of Intelligence and Love through the vast areas of the Universe.

Nothing entirely new happens under the Sun ; causes lead to new causes and effects precede these. Prophetic intuitions are but the result of a consideration of the analogies between the past and the future, read in that luminous volume composed of such mobile yet incorruptible characters as are the waves of the sea.

Hence it follows, that to divine—is to see.

Each man bears his earthly future in his natural character, and he has his character imprinted on his face and in his hands, in his natural movements, in his glances and his voice.

Each personal will has at its disposal three modes of force—moral power, instinctive power, and physical energy. Moral power is that solidarity which exists between all truly spiritual souls; instinctive power is the solidarity given by the sympathies and antipathies existing in the magnetic aura; while physical energy is the solidarity subsisting between the impulses and resistances of material substances. To each of these forces there is a corresponding form of life.

The middle or Instinctive force acts upon us without our active participation when our Moral force is in abeyance, and when one desires to give it free play one must slumber, or at least sleep more or less.

There is a voluntary slumber, as there is an involuntary or physiological sleep. Voluntary slumber is somewhat lucid, because it does not absolutely break away from reminiscence.

————

Prophecy and Thaumaturgy are Natural faculties.

Tho Re-animation of the Dead in the case of certain men and under certain circumstances is not a thing naturally impossible. At the moment of death the soul finds itself free from, yet near, the earthy tenement it has just left, and if the really vital organs have not been destroyed, it can be recalled by one whose will has tremendous force. Death is only absolute when the vital organs have lost their integrity.

Examples of re-animation are not infrequent, but when they occur the occurrence of death is denied, and the facts observed are explained by saying that the person was only in a trance or lethargy.

To deny that death has occurred in these cases may be permissible, but public opinion should have the courage of its convictions and should always deny it.

O thou who art now wise, thou hast been an infant; what has become of that infant? it has passed away, but you still live.

You have been a youth, he has passed away, but you are still with us. You were once a young man; what has become of that young man? you still live. You are now a man of full years, or perhaps even an old man; what will become of you, old man? You will die, but you will exist for ever. Is it the corpse which impresses you with terror? Yet each of your stages of development has left its corpse, only you do not happen to have seen it. Only believe then that your last corpse will not be appreciable by you, and so you may rest in a peaceful immortality.

You have but to undergo one more transformation before you remount to that source of life from which you once sprang.

Transformation results from eternal motion, which is the essential law of vitality; check this and enforce a stability at any stage of evolution, and you create a real death.

––––––

Behold thyself then, by natural law, immortal. Would you then be for ever the slave of secondary causes, or will you become their controller?

Will you submit to them, or will you choose the high alternative of directing them?

If you will become a Master, set free your spirit by relying on the Hermetic Stone, and exercise your Will Power through the Word transmuted into action. Join to an Intelligence, really set free, an all-powerful Will, and you will find yourself Master of the powers of the Elements. L. P. D.

Liberty, Power, Despotism. Power is the correct equilibrium between Despotism and Liberty. This is the solution of the Enigma of three letters which Cagliostro the Initiate formulated to represent the Kabalah of political and social stability.

Liberty is Chokmah.

Despotism is Binah.

Power beneficent is Kether.

Liberty is Gedulah.

Despotism is Geburah.

Power beneficent is Tiphereth.

Liberty is Netzach.

Despotism is Hod.

Power beneficent is in Yesod.

In the essence of the First Cause, Liberty has Necessity as a counterpoise; this Necessity is the despotism of Supreme Reason, and resulting from this equilbrium is a Wise and Absolute Power.

If you seek to be absolute, be first wise; and if you are wise, be then absolute. To be a Master you must be free; to be free you must have attained the mastery of yourself.

Liberty is Jakin.

Despotism is Boaz.

Power is represented by the Temple Gate which was between them.

Four phrases constitute and include all that is required for the possession of High Magical Power.

To know.

To dare.

To will.

To keep silence.

Knowledge is represented by the Human head of the Sphynx.

Courage, by its Eagle's wings.

Will, by the Lion's claws, and the loins of the Bull.

Secrecy, by its stony silence and by the hidden answer to its enigma.

When the pupil has grasped the meaning of, and can carry into practice, these four requirements, he may then receive permission to Love.

———

Every force corresponds to all forces, and may become all powerful in the hands of one who knows how to direct and use it.

Each form of weakness has a similarity to all weaknesses, and may become a slave to one who is strong and knows how to avail himself of it. Through the knowledge of this secret, the Magus commands the forces alike of heaven and hell, and they can but be submissive to his Will.

Realise clearly that an intelligence which is Free is of necessity both just and wise. Nero and Caligula were possessed of despotic will, but their intelligence was not free ; intoxicated with absolute power, they were attacked by vertigo. Absolute will power un-

guided by a right Reason is the quintessence of the
Devil; and here is the explanation of the secrets of
Black Magic, which lead to madness of mind and
poisoning of body. Hence the sorcerer is said to
give himself to the Devil, and in the end the Devil
will wring his neck.

You will now need to learn the last secret of
magical force and the final grade of human will
power.

It is Resistance to the Universal Attraction; this
is the conquest of nature, it is the Royal Authority
of Soul over Body—it is Continence. To have the
power and opportunity to do what gives pleasure, yet
to abstain because one wills it; this shows the Royal
power of Soul over body.

Happy is the man who can be so placed, and yet so
act: thus it is that the most sublime use of liberty is
absolute obedience. Without obedience no society can
continue to exist. This is why the Magi worshipped
the Christ in the stable at Bethlehem. Christ, that
son of God, greatest of initiates, and the last initiator.

But Christ had, as all great teachers have had, one
teaching for the people and also an esoteric doctrine.
To John, the beloved disciple, he confided the deepest
mysteries of the Holy Kabalah; and John in after

years revealed or reveiled them in his Apocalypse, which is indeed a synthesis of all earlier magical, prophetic, and Kabalistic works.

The Apocalypse requires as its key or Clavicula the Wheel of Ezekiel, which is itself explained by the hieroglyphs of the Tarot.

NOTES.

This final card, numbered 21 in the actual Tarot Trumps, and called Le Monde, represents an angelic or human figure floating in the air, almost nude, and holding a short wand in each hand. The figure is more female than male. Around her is an oval garland of leaves, and outside of this, at the four corners, are placed the Kerubic emblems of a man, lion, eagle, and bull. This figure, says Lévi, is Truth, and the mystical meaning is the Microcosm, or the *resumé* of all in all.

Christian draws the garland circular, and as formed of roses ; the Kerubim are placed at the four cardinal points, and not at the angles of the design ; he says its meaning is the Eternal Reward of a life well spent.

NOTE BY THE EDITOR

THE very curious manuscript volume, from which the preceding pages have been translated, concludes with a passage which appears to retract the whole of the foregoing instruction. It is a very notable illustration of the *second mind* of its author. Mr. Waite, who published an English translation of much that Lévi has written, has in his Preface called especial attention to the evidence that Lévi was drawn in a most mysterious fashion in two different directions by opposing forces. From his early training he tended to be a devout Catholic; from his Hebrew studies he became a Kabalist and a Magician. So even in this short occult treatise we find him, after carefully giving magical instruction through twenty-two chapters, making at its end a solemn recantation, and pointing out that the duty of a Christian is to the Church of Christ, which is the best and highest aim to which a man can attain.

THE CONCLUSION

By ÉLIPHAZ LÉVI

ONE last word remains to be said. When the
Temple is rebuilt, there will be no more sacrifice upon
its High places. Centuries have passed since Hermes
and Zoroaster lived and taught. A voice greater
than that of the Soul of the World has imposed
silence upon the Oracles.

The Word has been made Flesh; a new symbol of
salvation by holy water has replaced the magical
ceremonies of the day of Luna. The sacrifices to
Samael on the day of Mars are surpassed by the
heroic severities of penitence.

The sign of the Gift of Tongues and the Christian
code have replaced the sacrifices to Mercury.

The day once sacred to Jupiter is now devoted to
the sign of the Kingdom of God in man by the
transubstantiation of love under the forms of bread
and wine.

Anael has vanquished Venus : Lilith and Nahemah
are consigned to Hades, and the sacred rite of
marriage gives divine approval to the alliances of
men and women.

Lastly, extreme unction, which prepares a man for a death of peace, has replaced the sad offerings of Saturn; and the priesthood of light gives forth illumination on the day sacred to the Sun.

Glory be to the Christ, who has brought to their completion the symbols of the Ancient Mysteries, and who has prepared the reign of knowledge by faith. Will you now be greater than all Magi? Hide away your science in the recesses of your mind. Become a Christian, simple and docile; be a faithful servant of the Church, believe, mortify yourself, and obey.

OCCULT AND RELIGIOUS MAXIMS

From the MSS. of ÉLIPHAZ LÉVI

Every idle word is a fault.

Show your learning by your actions.

The Word is Life, and the First Principle of Life.

The quality of a life is shown by its actions.

An idle word is either without meaning or is of the nature of a lie.

An idle word in religious matters is a sin.

He who is content with idle words is as if he were dead.

He who does not make his worship manifest has no religion.

Better is superstition than impiety.

God judges actions rather than vain thoughts.

He who is religious will do works which accord with the Word of his religion; he who has no religion and believes not in any word, yet he also must be judged by his actions, for to every man shall it be according to his works.

True religion is that which showeth a form of worship which is pure and living; the perfection of worship, however, lieth in self-sacrifice, which is complete and enduring.

The beauty of self-sacrifice is taught in the Church of Christ, Catholic and Roman; and it is an article of faith, that any one who denies himself and takes up this cross, and follows the Mediator to the Altar, assumes at once the offices both of Priest and Victim.

No man ever saw GOD at any time.

Before the dawn of the Microcosm, Azoth was the Flying Eagle and the Royal Lion; it was the Mastodon of the Earth and the Leviathan of the Sea. When the human-headed Sphynx appeared—Azoth became Man among men, and Spirits among Elementals. Every substance can and should become Azoth by adaptation.

In Azoth is the Principle of the Light, which is the Quintessence of Splendour and Gold. This is the grand Secret of universal Transmutation.

No man has ever seen the Light; but we see by reason of it those objects which reflect the light.

There is nothing occult which shall not be known : there is nothing concealed which shall not be revealed.

The Kingdom of God is within us.

Initiation passes from East to West.
Intelligence passes from South to North.
Power passes from North to South.

The Word is the garment of the Truth.

God wields not absolute, but regulated power.

To tell the Truth to those who cannot understand
it, is to lie to them. To unveil the Truth to such
persons is to profane it.

THE END

Printed by BALLANTYNE, HANSON & Co.
Edinburgh and London

www.ingramcontent.com/pod-product-compliance
Ingram Content Group UK Ltd.
Pitfield, Milton Keynes, MK11 3LW, UK
UKHW042151280225
455719UK00001B/267